# Fix Your Focus

## A 52-WEEK GUIDE TO HELP YOU PUT GOD FIRST

SHELBY TURNER

## HOW TO USE THIS RESOURCE

Every week, there are tasks to be done, schedules to be kept, and needs to be met. Each week also requires time to connect to God and His Word, the Bible. Hebrews 12:1-2 tells us the life of faith is like a race—it will have many obstacles and require significant effort. To run this race well, we must fix our focus on Jesus, who is the source and perfecter of our faith.

Use this resource at the start of each week to fix your focus on Jesus and help organize your tasks and to-do lists. The sections of this booklet will lead you to journal, pray, meditate on Scripture, practice gratitude, and engage in spiritual disciplines each and every week. *Fix Your Focus* is designed to be used with a journal and a planner or calendar.

The spiritual growth section contains four different spiritual growth focuses: Serve, Rest, Fast, and Fellowship. Each week's prompts will feature just one of these focuses, and they will rotate every week. For additional information on the importance of practicing service, rest, fasting, and fellowship, continue reading.

Each week's entry concludes with a gospel-centered affirmation. This is a short and simple statement that you can easily remember and repeat to remind yourself of the beauty and truth of the gospel.

## SPIRITUAL GROWTH

Spiritual disciplines are practices that help us grow to maturity in our faith. Choosing to routinely engage in spiritual disciplines can help us prioritize the things of God and obey His commands daily. This resource encourages you to engage in service, rest, fasting, and fellowship. Read the following descriptions to learn and understand how you can incorporate these disciplines into your weeks. Verses for further reading are provided with each description.

## SERVE

God calls Christ-followers to serve others with their time, resources, prayers, and finances. Serving others is not about giving the most or being recognized—it is about stewarding what God has given you in a way that aligns with Scripture. Scripture calls Christians to care for those who are in need of food, shelter, comfort, and justice.

*Scripture: Proverbs 19:17, Acts 20:35, Matthew 5:16, Hebrews 6:10, Philippians 2:4*

## REST

Throughout Scripture, God prescribes rest for His people. God created the world in six days then rested on the seventh day of the creation story, declaring the day of rest as holy. Rest is worship to God when it is done God's way. In Exodus, God commanded the Israelites to rest from their secular work one day a week. That special day of rest was called the Sabbath. In the New Testament, Jesus modeled rest by often withdrawing from crowded places to commune quietly with His Father. We, too, can honor God by choosing to rest.

*Scripture: Genesis 2:2-3, Exodus 20:8-11, Matthew 11:28-30, Mark 6:31*

## FAST

Fasting is choosing to abstain from food or anything else for a set period of time to focus more intently on God and His goodness. When we choose to fast, we deprive ourselves of something good so that we will rely in a greater measure upon God, who gives all good things. You may choose to fast from all food, just one meal, sugar, television, social media, or anything else. Consider increasing the time you spend praying and reading the Bible for the duration of your fast.

*Scripture: Acts 14:23, Daniel 9:1-3, Daniel 10:1-3, Joel 2:12, Psalm 35:13-14, Luke 4:1-4*

## FELLOWSHIP

Christians are not meant to live life alone. In the Bible, we are described as brothers and sisters, the body of Christ, and a global Church, all working together for the same mission. We are told not to neglect meeting together with other believers and to continually encourage and pray for one another. Fellowship with other Christians is essential to the health and growth of our faith. Fellowship can look like meeting up for coffee, a dinner shared in your home, or a phone call with a friend.

*Scripture: Acts 2:42, 1 John 1:3-7, Matthew 18:20, Hebrews 10:24-25*

THE LIFE OF FAITH

IS LIKE A RACE—

IT WILL HAVE

MANY OBSTACLES

AND REQUIRE

SIGNIFICANT EFFORT.

IN ORDER TO
RUN THIS RACE WELL,
WE NEED TO FIX OUR
FOCUS ON JESUS,
WHO IS THE SOURCE
AND PERFECTER
OF OUR FAITH.

## JOURNAL

*When planning a week, it is common to think of our to-do lists, but do we also consider the state of our souls? Take a moment to journal about your fears, joys, worries, desires, and stressors.*

## PRAYER

*Use the following prayer prompts to have a conversation with God about the week ahead.*

▶ **LORD, YOU ARE...**

▶ **LORD, I FEEL...**

▶ **LORD, HELP ME WITH...**

▶ **LORD, FORGIVE ME FOR...**

*Make a note of four or five people you are specifically praying for. It may be helpful to list their names in your planner so that you remember to pray for them throughout the week.*

○ _____

○ _____

○ _____

○ _____

○ _____

## SCRIPTURE MEDITATION

*Teach me to do your will, for you are my God.*
*May your gracious Spirit lead me on level ground.*
**PSALM 143:10**

▶ *Reflect on what this verse tells you about who God is.*

▶ *Think about what this verse tells you about who you are.*

▶ *Write this verse in your planner, or put it in a place where you will see it frequently. Throughout the week, consider how it should affect the way you live.*

## GRATITUDE

*Reflect on the ways God has shown His faithfulness to you over the last week. List five things you are thankful for.*

1. _____

2. _____

3. _____

4. _____

5. _____

## SPIRITUAL GROWTH | SERVE

*Who do you know that is in need? Think about what resources you have available to you (time, finances, prayer, etc.). Consider how you could help someone in need this week.*

## WEEK-AT-A-GLANCE CHECKLIST

*Whatever you do, do it from the heart, as something done for the Lord and not for people, knowing that you will receive the reward of an inheritance from the Lord. You serve the Lord Christ.*
*— Colossians 3:23-24*

- ○ MAKE A PLAN FOR WHEN YOU WILL PRAY AND READ YOUR BIBLE THIS WEEK.

- ○ ADD ANY UPCOMING EVENTS TO YOUR CALENDAR.

- ○ JOT DOWN A TO-DO LIST OF TASKS THAT MUST BE COMPLETED THIS WEEK.

- ○ MAKE A NOTE OF YOUR TOP THREE PRIORITIES THIS WEEK TO STAY ON TRACK.

## GOSPEL-CENTERED AFFIRMATION

*The Lord is my God.*
*He teaches and leads me by His Spirit.*

WEEK 02

## JOURNAL

*When planning a week, it is common to think of our to-do lists, but do we also consider the state of our souls? Take a moment to journal about your fears, joys, worries, desires, and stressors.*

## PRAYER

*Use the following prayer prompts to have a conversation with God about the week ahead.*

▶ **LORD, YOU ARE...**

▶ **LORD, I FEEL...**

▶ **LORD, HELP ME WITH...**

▶ **LORD, FORGIVE ME FOR...**

*Make a note of four or five people you are specifically praying for. It may be helpful to list their names in your planner so that you remember to pray for them throughout the week.*

○ _____

○ _____

○ _____

○ _____

○ _____

## SCRIPTURE MEDITATION

*Taste and see that the Lord is good. How happy is the person who takes refuge in him!*

**PSALM 34:8**

▶ *Reflect on what this verse tells you about who God is.*

▶ *Think about what this verse tells you about who you are.*

▶ *Write this verse in your planner, or put it in a place where you will see it frequently. Throughout the week, consider how it should affect the way you live.*

## GRATITUDE

*Reflect on the ways God has shown His faithfulness to you over the last week. List five things you are thankful for.*

1. _____

2. _____

3. _____

4. _____

5. _____

## SPIRITUAL GROWTH | REST

*Think about what observing a Sabbath rest looks like to you. Make a plan to intentionally rest this week.*

## WEEK-AT-A-GLANCE CHECKLIST

*Whatever you do, do it from the heart, as something done for the Lord and not for people, knowing that you will receive the reward of an inheritance from the Lord. You serve the Lord Christ.*
*—Colossians 3:23-24*

○ **MAKE A PLAN FOR WHEN YOU WILL PRAY AND READ YOUR BIBLE THIS WEEK.**

○ **ADD ANY UPCOMING EVENTS TO YOUR CALENDAR.**

○ **JOT DOWN A TO-DO LIST OF TASKS THAT MUST BE COMPLETED THIS WEEK.**

○ **MAKE A NOTE OF YOUR TOP THREE PRIORITIES THIS WEEK TO STAY ON TRACK.**

## GOSPEL-CENTERED AFFIRMATION

*When I trust in God, I experience joy.*

WEEK 03

## JOURNAL

*When planning a week, it is common to think of our to-do lists, but do we also consider the state of our souls? Take a moment to journal about your fears, joys, worries, desires, and stressors.*

## PRAYER

*Use the following prayer prompts to have a conversation with God about the week ahead.*

▶ **LORD, YOU ARE...**

▶ **LORD, I FEEL...**

▶ **LORD, HELP ME WITH...**

▶ **LORD, FORGIVE ME FOR...**

*Make a note of four or five people you are specifically praying for. It may be helpful to list their names in your planner so that you remember to pray for them throughout the week.*

○ _____

○ _____

○ _____

○ _____

○ _____

## SCRIPTURE MEDITATION

> *Rejoice in hope; be patient in affliction;*
> *be persistent in prayer.*
> **ROMANS 12:12**

▶ *Reflect on what this verse tells you about who God is.*

▶ *Think about what this verse tells you about who you are.*

▶ *Write this verse in your planner, or put it in a place where you will see it frequently. Throughout the week, consider how it should affect the way you live.*

## GRATITUDE

*Reflect on the ways God has shown His faithfulness to you over the last week. List five things you are thankful for.*

1. _____

2. _____

3. _____

4. _____

5. _____

## SPIRITUAL GROWTH | FAST

*Consider fasting from something this week in order to focus on your need for God. What could you fast from? What would be the duration and frequency of your fast? Make a plan for how you will replace your fasted item with the pursuit of God and His Word.*

## WEEK-AT-A-GLANCE CHECKLIST

*Whatever you do, do it from the heart, as something done for the Lord and not for people, knowing that you will receive the reward of an inheritance from the Lord. You serve the Lord Christ.*
*— Colossians 3:23-24*

○ **MAKE A PLAN FOR WHEN YOU WILL PRAY AND READ YOUR BIBLE THIS WEEK.**

○ **ADD ANY UPCOMING EVENTS TO YOUR CALENDAR.**

○ **JOT DOWN A TO-DO LIST OF TASKS THAT MUST BE COMPLETED THIS WEEK.**

○ **MAKE A NOTE OF YOUR TOP THREE PRIORITIES THIS WEEK TO STAY ON TRACK.**

## GOSPEL-CENTERED AFFIRMATION

*I can patiently and prayerfully endure hardship because my hope is in Jesus.*

## JOURNAL

*When planning a week, it is common to think of our to-do lists, but do we also consider the state of our souls? Take a moment to journal about your fears, joys, worries, desires, and stressors.*

## PRAYER

*Use the following prayer prompts to have a conversation with God about the week ahead.*

▶ **LORD, YOU ARE...**

▶ **LORD, I FEEL...**

▶ **LORD, HELP ME WITH...**

▶ **LORD, FORGIVE ME FOR...**

*Make a note of four or five people you are specifically praying for. It may be helpful to list their names in your planner so that you remember to pray for them throughout the week.*

○ _____

○ _____

○ _____

○ _____

○ _____

## SCRIPTURE MEDITATION

> *Humble yourselves, therefore, under the mighty hand of God, so that he may exalt you at the proper time, casting all your cares on him, because he cares about you.*
> **1 PETER 5:6-7**

▶ *Reflect on what these verses tell you about who God is.*

▶ *Think about what these verses tell you about who you are.*

▶ *Write these verses in your planner, or put them in a place where you will see them frequently. Throughout the week, consider how these verses should affect the way you live.*

## GRATITUDE

*Reflect on the ways God has shown His faithfulness to you over the last week. List five things you are thankful for.*

1. _____

2. _____

3. _____

4. _____

5. _____

## SPIRITUAL GROWTH | FELLOWSHIP

*Plan a time to fellowship with friends this week. Go ahead and reach out to them now to get it on the calendar.*

## WEEK-AT-A-GLANCE CHECKLIST

*Whatever you do, do it from the heart, as something done for the Lord and not for people, knowing that you will receive the reward of an inheritance from the Lord. You serve the Lord Christ.*
*—Colossians 3:23-24*

- ○ **MAKE A PLAN FOR WHEN YOU WILL PRAY AND READ YOUR BIBLE THIS WEEK.**

- ○ **ADD ANY UPCOMING EVENTS TO YOUR CALENDAR.**

- ○ **JOT DOWN A TO-DO LIST OF TASKS THAT MUST BE COMPLETED THIS WEEK.**

- ○ **MAKE A NOTE OF YOUR TOP THREE PRIORITIES THIS WEEK TO STAY ON TRACK.**

## GOSPEL-CENTERED AFFIRMATION

*I humbly yield my plans to God's will.*

## JOURNAL

*When planning a week, it is common to think of our to-do lists, but do we also consider the state of our souls? Take a moment to journal about your fears, joys, worries, desires, and stressors.*

## PRAYER

*Use the following prayer prompts to have a conversation with God about the week ahead.*

▶ **LORD, YOU ARE...**

▶ **LORD, I FEEL...**

▶ **LORD, HELP ME WITH...**

▶ **LORD, FORGIVE ME FOR...**

*Make a note of four or five people you are specifically praying for. It may be helpful to list their names in your planner so that you remember to pray for them throughout the week.*

○ _____

○ _____

○ _____

○ _____

○ _____

## SCRIPTURE MEDITATION

*You are my shelter and my shield;*
*I put my hope in your word.*
**PSALM 119:114**

▶ *Reflect on what this verse tells you about who God is.*

▶ *Think about what this verse tells you about who you are.*

▶ *Write this verse in your planner, or put it in a place where you will see it frequently. Throughout the week, consider how it should affect the way you live.*

## GRATITUDE

*Reflect on the ways God has shown His faithfulness to you over the last week. List five things you are thankful for.*

1. _____

2. _____

3. _____

4. _____

5. _____

## SPIRITUAL GROWTH | SERVE

*Who do you know that is in need? Think about what resources you have available to you (time, finances, prayer, etc.). Consider how you could serve those in need this week.*

## WEEK-AT-A-GLANCE CHECKLIST

*Whatever you do, do it from the heart, as something done for the Lord and not for people, knowing that you will receive the reward of an inheritance from the Lord. You serve the Lord Christ.*
—*Colossians 3:23-24*

- ○ MAKE A PLAN FOR WHEN YOU WILL PRAY AND READ YOUR BIBLE THIS WEEK.

- ○ ADD ANY UPCOMING EVENTS TO YOUR CALENDAR.

- ○ JOT DOWN A TO-DO LIST OF TASKS THAT MUST BE COMPLETED THIS WEEK.

- ○ MAKE A NOTE OF YOUR TOP THREE PRIORITIES THIS WEEK TO STAY ON TRACK.

## GOSPEL-CENTERED AFFIRMATION

*All my hope is in the Lord.
He faithfully keeps His Word.*

WEEK 06

## JOURNAL

*When planning a week, it is common to think of our to-do lists, but do we also consider the state of our souls? Take a moment to journal about your fears, joys, worries, desires, and stressors.*

## PRAYER

*Use the following prayer prompts to have a conversation with God about the week ahead.*

▶ **LORD, YOU ARE...**

▶ **LORD, I FEEL...**

▶ **LORD, HELP ME WITH...**

▶ **LORD, FORGIVE ME FOR...**

*Make a note of four or five people you are specifically praying for. It may be helpful to list their names in your planner so that you remember to pray for them throughout the week.*

○ _____

○ _____

○ _____

○ _____

○ _____

## SCRIPTURE MEDITATION

*I am the vine; you are the branches. The one who remains in me and I in him produces much fruit, because you can do nothing without me.*

**JOHN 15:5**

▶ *Reflect on what this verse tells you about who God is.*

▶ *Think about what this verse tells you about who you are.*

▶ *Write this verse in your planner, or put it in a place where you will see it frequently. Throughout the week, consider how it should affect the way you live.*

## GRATITUDE

*Reflect on the ways God has shown His faithfulness to you over the last week. List five things you are thankful for.*

1. _____

2. _____

3. _____

4. _____

5. _____

## SPIRITUAL GROWTH | REST

*Think about what observing a Sabbath rest looks like to you.*
*Make a plan to intentionally rest this week.*

## WEEK-AT-A-GLANCE CHECKLIST

*Whatever you do, do it from the heart, as something done for*
*the Lord and not for people, knowing that you will receive the*
*reward of an inheritance from the Lord. You serve the Lord Christ.*
*—Colossians 3:23-24*

○ **MAKE A PLAN FOR WHEN YOU WILL PRAY**
**AND READ YOUR BIBLE THIS WEEK.**

○ **ADD ANY UPCOMING EVENTS TO**
**YOUR CALENDAR.**

○ **JOT DOWN A TO-DO LIST OF TASKS THAT**
**MUST BE COMPLETED THIS WEEK.**

○ **MAKE A NOTE OF YOUR TOP THREE**
**PRIORITIES THIS WEEK TO STAY ON TRACK.**

## GOSPEL-CENTERED AFFIRMATION

*Anything good that I do is because*
*I am connected to the Lord.*

## JOURNAL

*When planning a week, it is common to think of our to-do lists, but do we also consider the state of our souls? Take a moment to journal about your fears, joys, worries, desires, and stressors.*

## PRAYER

*Use the following prayer prompts to have a conversation with God about the week ahead.*

▶ **LORD, YOU ARE...**

▶ **LORD, I FEEL...**

▶ **LORD, HELP ME WITH...**

▶ **LORD, FORGIVE ME FOR...**

*Make a note of four or five people you are specifically praying for. It may be helpful to list their names in your planner so that you remember to pray for them throughout the week.*

○ _____

○ _____

○ _____

○ _____

○ _____

## SCRIPTURE MEDITATION

*Be merciful, just as your Father also is merciful.*

**LUKE 6:36**

▶ *Reflect on what this verse tells you about who God is.*

▶ *Think about what this verse tells you about who you are.*

▶ *Write this verse in your planner, or put it in a place where you will see it frequently. Throughout the week, consider how it should affect the way you live.*

## GRATITUDE

*Reflect on the ways God has shown His faithfulness to you over the last week. List five things you are thankful for.*

1. _____

2. _____

3. _____

4. _____

5. _____

## SPIRITUAL GROWTH | FAST

*Consider fasting from something this week in order to focus on your need for God. What could you fast from? What would be the duration and frequency of your fast? Make a plan for how you will replace your fasted item with the pursuit of God and His Word.*

## WEEK-AT-A-GLANCE CHECKLIST

*Whatever you do, do it from the heart, as something done for the Lord and not for people, knowing that you will receive the reward of an inheritance from the Lord. You serve the Lord Christ.*
*—Colossians 3:23-24*

- ○ MAKE A PLAN FOR WHEN YOU WILL PRAY AND READ YOUR BIBLE THIS WEEK.

- ○ ADD ANY UPCOMING EVENTS TO YOUR CALENDAR.

- ○ JOT DOWN A TO-DO LIST OF TASKS THAT MUST BE COMPLETED THIS WEEK.

- ○ MAKE A NOTE OF YOUR TOP THREE PRIORITIES THIS WEEK TO STAY ON TRACK.

## GOSPEL-CENTERED AFFIRMATION

*God has been merciful to me, and He asks me to be merciful toward others.*

WEEK 08

## JOURNAL

*When planning a week, it is common to think of our to-do lists, but do we also consider the state of our souls? Take a moment to journal about your fears, joys, worries, desires, and stressors.*

## PRAYER

*Use the following prayer prompts to have a conversation with God about the week ahead.*

▶ **LORD, YOU ARE...**

▶ **LORD, I FEEL...**

▶ **LORD, HELP ME WITH...**

▶ **LORD, FORGIVE ME FOR...**

*Make a note of four or five people you are specifically praying for. It may be helpful to list their names in your planner so that you remember to pray for them throughout the week.*

○ _____

○ _____

○ _____

○ _____

○ _____

## SCRIPTURE MEDITATION

*Finally brothers and sisters, whatever is true, whatever is honorable, whatever is just, whatever is pure, whatever is lovely, whatever is commendable— if there is any moral excellence and if there is anything praiseworthy—dwell on these things.*

**PHILIPPIANS 4:8**

▶ *Reflect on what this verse tells you about who God is.*

▶ *Think about what this verse tells you about who you are.*

▶ *Write this verse in your planner, or put it in a place where you will see it frequently. Throughout the week, consider how it should affect the way you live.*

## GRATITUDE

*Reflect on the ways God has shown His faithfulness to you over the last week. List five things you are thankful for.*

1. _____

2. _____

3. _____

4. _____

5. _____

## SPIRITUAL GROWTH | FELLOWSHIP

*Plan a time to fellowship with friends this week. Go ahead and reach out to them now to get it on the calendar.*

## WEEK-AT-A-GLANCE CHECKLIST

*Whatever you do, do it from the heart, as something done for the Lord and not for people, knowing that you will receive the reward of an inheritance from the Lord. You serve the Lord Christ.*
—*Colossians 3:23-24*

○ MAKE A PLAN FOR WHEN YOU WILL PRAY AND READ YOUR BIBLE THIS WEEK.

○ ADD ANY UPCOMING EVENTS TO YOUR CALENDAR.

○ JOT DOWN A TO-DO LIST OF TASKS THAT MUST BE COMPLETED THIS WEEK.

○ MAKE A NOTE OF YOUR TOP THREE PRIORITIES THIS WEEK TO STAY ON TRACK.

## GOSPEL-CENTERED AFFIRMATION

*I choose to think on what the Lord calls praiseworthy.*

WEEK 09

## JOURNAL

*When planning a week, it is common to think of our to-do lists, but do we also consider the state of our souls? Take a moment to journal about your fears, joys, worries, desires, and stressors.*

## PRAYER

*Use the following prayer prompts to have a conversation with God about the week ahead.*

▶ **LORD, YOU ARE...**

▶ **LORD, I FEEL...**

▶ **LORD, HELP ME WITH...**

▶ **LORD, FORGIVE ME FOR...**

*Make a note of four or five people you are specifically praying for. It may be helpful to list their names in your planner so that you remember to pray for them throughout the week.*

○ _____

○ _____

○ _____

○ _____

○ _____

## SCRIPTURE MEDITATION

*You forgave your people's guilt;*
*you covered all their sin.*

**PSALM 85:2**

▶ *Reflect on what this verse tells you about who God is.*

▶ *Think about what this verse tells you about who you are.*

▶ *Write this verse in your planner, or put it in a place where you will see it frequently. Throughout the week, consider how it should affect the way you live.*

## GRATITUDE

*Reflect on the ways God has shown His faithfulness to you over the last week. List five things you are thankful for.*

1. _____

2. _____

3. _____

4. _____

5. _____

## SPIRITUAL GROWTH | SERVE

*Who do you know that is in need? Think about what resources you have available to you (time, finances, prayer, etc.). Consider how you could serve someone in need this week.*

## WEEK-AT-A-GLANCE CHECKLIST

*Whatever you do, do it from the heart, as something done for the Lord and not for people, knowing that you will receive the reward of an inheritance from the Lord. You serve the Lord Christ.*
*—Colossians 3:23-24*

○ **MAKE A PLAN FOR WHEN YOU WILL PRAY AND READ YOUR BIBLE THIS WEEK.**

○ **ADD ANY UPCOMING EVENTS TO YOUR CALENDAR.**

○ **JOT DOWN A TO-DO LIST OF TASKS THAT MUST BE COMPLETED THIS WEEK.**

○ **MAKE A NOTE OF YOUR TOP THREE PRIORITIES THIS WEEK TO STAY ON TRACK.**

## GOSPEL-CENTERED AFFIRMATION

*In Christ, I am forgiven.*

## JOURNAL

*When planning a week, it is common to think of our to-do lists, but do we also consider the state of our souls? Take a moment to journal about your fears, joys, worries, desires, and stressors.*

## PRAYER

*Use the following prayer prompts to have a conversation with God about the week ahead.*

▶ **LORD, YOU ARE...**

▶ **LORD, I FEEL...**

▶ **LORD, HELP ME WITH...**

▶ **LORD, FORGIVE ME FOR...**

*Make a note of four or five people you are specifically praying for. It may be helpful to list their names in your planner so that you remember to pray for them throughout the week.*

○ _____

○ _____

○ _____

○ _____

○ _____

## SCRIPTURE MEDITATION

*Therefore, whatever you want others to
do for you, do also the same for them,
for this is the Law and the Prophets.*
**MATTHEW 7:12**

▶ *Reflect on what this verse tells you about who God is.*

▶ *Think about what this verse tells you about who you are.*

▶ *Write this verse in your planner, or put it in a place
where you will see it frequently. Throughout the week,
consider how it should affect the way you live.*

## GRATITUDE

*Reflect on the ways God has shown His faithfulness to you
over the last week. List five things you are thankful for.*

1. _____

2. _____

3. _____

4. _____

5. _____

## SPIRITUAL GROWTH | REST

*Think about what observing a Sabbath rest looks like to you. Make a plan to intentionally rest this week.*

## WEEK-AT-A-GLANCE CHECKLIST

*Whatever you do, do it from the heart, as something done for the Lord and not for people, knowing that you will receive the reward of an inheritance from the Lord. You serve the Lord Christ.*
—*Colossians 3:23-24*

○ **MAKE A PLAN FOR WHEN YOU WILL PRAY AND READ YOUR BIBLE THIS WEEK.**

○ **ADD ANY UPCOMING EVENTS TO YOUR CALENDAR.**

○ **JOT DOWN A TO-DO LIST OF TASKS THAT MUST BE COMPLETED THIS WEEK.**

○ **MAKE A NOTE OF YOUR TOP THREE PRIORITIES THIS WEEK TO STAY ON TRACK.**

## GOSPEL-CENTERED AFFIRMATION

*Following the example of Jesus, I will do for others what I want others to do for me.*

WEEK 11

## JOURNAL

*When planning a week, it is common to think of our to-do lists, but do we also consider the state of our souls? Take a moment to journal about your fears, joys, worries, desires, and stressors.*

## PRAYER

*Use the following prayer prompts to have a conversation with God about the week ahead.*

▶ **LORD, YOU ARE...**

▶ **LORD, I FEEL...**

▶ **LORD, HELP ME WITH...**

▶ **LORD, FORGIVE ME FOR...**

*Make a note of four or five people you are specifically praying for. It may be helpful to list their names in your planner so that you remember to pray for them throughout the week.*

○ _____

○ _____

○ _____

○ _____

○ _____

## SCRIPTURE MEDITATION

*The Lord is near all who call out to him,*
*all who call out to him with integrity.*

**PSALM 145:18**

▶ *Reflect on what this verse tells you about who God is.*

▶ *Think about what this verse tells you about who you are.*

▶ *Write this verse in your planner, or put it in a place*
*where you will see it frequently. Throughout the week,*
*consider how it should affect the way you live.*

## GRATITUDE

*Reflect on the ways God has shown His faithfulness to you*
*over the last week. List five things you are thankful for.*

1. _____

2. _____

3. _____

4. _____

5. _____

## SPIRITUAL GROWTH | FAST

*Consider fasting from something this week in order to focus on your need for God. What could you fast from? What would be the duration and frequency of your fast? Make a plan for how you will replace your fasted item with the pursuit of God and His Word.*

## WEEK-AT-A-GLANCE CHECKLIST

*Whatever you do, do it from the heart, as something done for the Lord and not for people, knowing that you will receive the reward of an inheritance from the Lord. You serve the Lord Christ.*
*—Colossians 3:23-24*

○ MAKE A PLAN FOR WHEN YOU WILL PRAY
   AND READ YOUR BIBLE THIS WEEK.

○ ADD ANY UPCOMING EVENTS TO
   YOUR CALENDAR.

○ JOT DOWN A TO-DO LIST OF TASKS THAT
   MUST BE COMPLETED THIS WEEK.

○ MAKE A NOTE OF YOUR TOP THREE
   PRIORITIES THIS WEEK TO STAY ON TRACK.

## GOSPEL-CENTERED AFFIRMATION

*The Lord is near; when I call, He hears.*

## JOURNAL

*When planning a week, it is common to think of our to-do lists, but do we also consider the state of our souls? Take a moment to journal about your fears, joys, worries, desires, and stressors.*

## PRAYER

*Use the following prayer prompts to have a conversation with God about the week ahead.*

▶ **LORD, YOU ARE...**

▶ **LORD, I FEEL...**

▶ **LORD, HELP ME WITH...**

▶ **LORD, FORGIVE ME FOR...**

*Make a note of four or five people you are specifically praying for. It may be helpful to list their names in your planner so that you remember to pray for them throughout the week.*

○ _____

○ _____

○ _____

○ _____

○ _____

## SCRIPTURE MEDITATION

> *Then he said to his disciples, "The harvest is abundant, but the workers are few. Therefore, pray to the Lord of the harvest to send out workers into his harvest."*
> **MATTHEW 9:37-38**

▶ *Reflect on what these verses tell you about who God is.*

▶ *Think about what these verses tell you about who you are.*

▶ *Write these verses in your planner, or put them in a place where you will see them frequently. Throughout the week, consider how these verses should affect the way you live.*

## GRATITUDE

*Reflect on the ways God has shown His faithfulness to you over the last week. List five things you are thankful for.*

1. _____

2. _____

3. _____

4. _____

5. _____

## SPIRITUAL GROWTH | FELLOWSHIP

*Plan a time to fellowship with friends this week. Go ahead and reach out to them now to get it on the calendar.*

## WEEK-AT-A-GLANCE CHECKLIST

*Whatever you do, do it from the heart, as something done for the Lord and not for people, knowing that you will receive the reward of an inheritance from the Lord. You serve the Lord Christ.*
*—Colossians 3:23-24*

- ○ MAKE A PLAN FOR WHEN YOU WILL PRAY AND READ YOUR BIBLE THIS WEEK.

- ○ ADD ANY UPCOMING EVENTS TO YOUR CALENDAR.

- ○ JOT DOWN A TO-DO LIST OF TASKS THAT MUST BE COMPLETED THIS WEEK.

- ○ MAKE A NOTE OF YOUR TOP THREE PRIORITIES THIS WEEK TO STAY ON TRACK.

## GOSPEL-CENTERED AFFIRMATION

*I will engage in spreading the gospel message.*

## JOURNAL

*When planning a week, it is common to think of our to-do lists, but do we also consider the state of our souls? Take a moment to journal about your fears, joys, worries, desires, and stressors.*

## PRAYER

*Use the following prayer prompts to have a conversation with God about the week ahead.*

▶ **LORD, YOU ARE...**

▶ **LORD, I FEEL...**

▶ **LORD, HELP ME WITH...**

▶ **LORD, FORGIVE ME FOR...**

*Make a note of four or five people you are specifically praying for. It may be helpful to list their names in your planner so that you remember to pray for them throughout the week.*

○ _____

○ _____

○ _____

○ _____

○ _____

## SCRIPTURE MEDITATION

*One who is righteous has many adversities,*
*but the Lord rescues him from them all.*

**PSALM 34:19**

▶ *Reflect on what this verse tells you about who God is.*

▶ *Think about what this verse tells you about who you are.*

▶ *Write this verse in your planner, or put it in a place*
*where you will see it frequently. Throughout the week,*
*consider how it should affect the way you live.*

## GRATITUDE

*Reflect on the ways God has shown His faithfulness to you*
*over the last week. List five things you are thankful for.*

1. _____

2. _____

3. _____

4. _____

5. _____

## SPIRITUAL GROWTH | SERVE

*Who do you know that is in need? Think about what resources you have available to you (time, finances, prayer, etc.). Consider how you could serve those in need this week.*

## WEEK-AT-A-GLANCE CHECKLIST

*Whatever you do, do it from the heart, as something done for the Lord and not for people, knowing that you will receive the reward of an inheritance from the Lord. You serve the Lord Christ.*
*—Colossians 3:23-24*

○ **MAKE A PLAN FOR WHEN YOU WILL PRAY AND READ YOUR BIBLE THIS WEEK.**

○ **ADD ANY UPCOMING EVENTS TO YOUR CALENDAR.**

○ **JOT DOWN A TO-DO LIST OF TASKS THAT MUST BE COMPLETED THIS WEEK.**

○ **MAKE A NOTE OF YOUR TOP THREE PRIORITIES THIS WEEK TO STAY ON TRACK.**

## GOSPEL-CENTERED AFFIRMATION

*I will face adversity, but the Lord will rescue me.*

**WEEK 14**

## JOURNAL

*When planning a week, it is common to think of our to-do lists, but do we also consider the state of our souls? Take a moment to journal about your fears, joys, worries, desires, and stressors.*

## PRAYER

*Use the following prayer prompts to have a conversation with God about the week ahead.*

▶ **LORD, YOU ARE...**

▶ **LORD, I FEEL...**

▶ **LORD, HELP ME WITH...**

▶ **LORD, FORGIVE ME FOR...**

*Make a note of four or five people you are specifically praying for. It may be helpful to list their names in your planner so that you remember to pray for them throughout the week.*

○ _____

○ _____

○ _____

○ _____

○ _____

## SCRIPTURE MEDITATION

*Blessed are those who mourn,*
*for they will be comforted.*

**MATTHEW 5:4**

▶ *Reflect on what this verse tells you about who God is.*

▶ *Think about what this verse tells you about who you are.*

▶ *Write this verse in your planner, or put it in a place where you will see it frequently. Throughout the week, consider how it should affect the way you live.*

## GRATITUDE

*Reflect on the ways God has shown His faithfulness to you over the last week. List five things you are thankful for.*

1. _____

2. _____

3. _____

4. _____

5. _____

## SPIRITUAL GROWTH | REST

*Think about what observing a Sabbath rest looks like to you. Make a plan to intentionally rest this week.*

## WEEK-AT-A-GLANCE CHECKLIST

*Whatever you do, do it from the heart, as something done for the Lord and not for people, knowing that you will receive the reward of an inheritance from the Lord. You serve the Lord Christ.* —Colossians 3:23-24

○ MAKE A PLAN FOR WHEN YOU WILL PRAY AND READ YOUR BIBLE THIS WEEK.

○ ADD ANY UPCOMING EVENTS TO YOUR CALENDAR.

○ JOT DOWN A TO-DO LIST OF TASKS THAT MUST BE COMPLETED THIS WEEK.

○ MAKE A NOTE OF YOUR TOP THREE PRIORITIES THIS WEEK TO STAY ON TRACK.

## GOSPEL-CENTERED AFFIRMATION

*In my mourning, I find joy in God's comfort.*

# WEEK 15

## JOURNAL

*When planning a week, it is common to think of our to-do lists, but do we also consider the state of our souls? Take a moment to journal about your fears, joys, worries, desires, and stressors.*

## PRAYER

*Use the following prayer prompts to have a conversation with God about the week ahead.*

▶ **LORD, YOU ARE...**

▶ **LORD, I FEEL...**

▶ **LORD, HELP ME WITH...**

▶ **LORD, FORGIVE ME FOR...**

*Make a note of four or five people you are specifically praying for. It may be helpful to list their names in your planner so that you remember to pray for them throughout the week.*

○ _____

○ _____

○ _____

○ _____

○ _____

## SCRIPTURE MEDITATION

> *Unless the Lord builds a house, its builders*
> *labor over it in vain; unless the Lord watches*
> *over a city, the watchman stays alert in vain.*
> **PSALM 127:1**

▶ *Reflect on what this verse tells you about who God is.*

▶ *Think about what this verse tells you about who you are.*

▶ *Write this verse in your planner, or put it in a place*
*where you will see it frequently. Throughout the week,*
*consider how it should affect the way you live.*

## GRATITUDE

*Reflect on the ways God has shown His faithfulness to you*
*over the last week. List five things you are thankful for.*

1. _____

2. _____

3. _____

4. _____

5. _____

## SPIRITUAL GROWTH | FAST

*Consider fasting from something this week in order to focus on your need for God. What could you fast from? What would be the duration and frequency of your fast? Make a plan for how you will replace your fasted item with the pursuit of God and His Word.*

## WEEK-AT-A-GLANCE CHECKLIST

*Whatever you do, do it from the heart, as something done for the Lord and not for people, knowing that you will receive the reward of an inheritance from the Lord. You serve the Lord Christ.*
*— Colossians 3:23-24*

○ MAKE A PLAN FOR WHEN YOU WILL PRAY AND READ YOUR BIBLE THIS WEEK.

○ ADD ANY UPCOMING EVENTS TO YOUR CALENDAR.

○ JOT DOWN A TO-DO LIST OF TASKS THAT MUST BE COMPLETED THIS WEEK.

○ MAKE A NOTE OF YOUR TOP THREE PRIORITIES THIS WEEK TO STAY ON TRACK.

## GOSPEL-CENTERED AFFIRMATION

*It is the Lord, not human effort,*
*that makes any task successful.*

## JOURNAL

*When planning a week, it is common to think of our to-do lists, but do we also consider the state of our souls? Take a moment to journal about your fears, joys, worries, desires, and stressors.*

## PRAYER

*Use the following prayer prompts to have a conversation with God about the week ahead.*

▶ **LORD, YOU ARE...**

▶ **LORD, I FEEL...**

▶ **LORD, HELP ME WITH...**

▶ **LORD, FORGIVE ME FOR...**

*Make a note of four or five people you are specifically praying for. It may be helpful to list their names in your planner so that you remember to pray for them throughout the week.*

○ _____

○ _____

○ _____

○ _____

○ _____

## SCRIPTURE MEDITATION

*But seek first the kingdom of God and his righteousness, and all these things will be provided for you.*

**MATTHEW 6:33**

▶ *Reflect on what this verse tells you about who God is.*

▶ *Think about what this verse tells you about who you are.*

▶ *Write this verse in your planner, or put it in a place where you will see it frequently. Throughout the week, consider how it should affect the way you live.*

## GRATITUDE

*Reflect on the ways God has shown His faithfulness to you over the last week. List five things you are thankful for.*

1. _____

2. _____

3. _____

4. _____

5. _____

## SPIRITUAL GROWTH | FELLOWSHIP

*Plan a time to fellowship with friends this week. Go ahead and reach out to them now to get it on the calendar.*

## WEEK-AT-A-GLANCE CHECKLIST

*Whatever you do, do it from the heart, as something done for the Lord and not for people, knowing that you will receive the reward of an inheritance from the Lord. You serve the Lord Christ.*
*—Colossians 3:23-24*

○ **MAKE A PLAN FOR WHEN YOU WILL PRAY AND READ YOUR BIBLE THIS WEEK.**

○ **ADD ANY UPCOMING EVENTS TO YOUR CALENDAR.**

○ **JOT DOWN A TO-DO LIST OF TASKS THAT MUST BE COMPLETED THIS WEEK.**

○ **MAKE A NOTE OF YOUR TOP THREE PRIORITIES THIS WEEK TO STAY ON TRACK.**

## GOSPEL-CENTERED AFFIRMATION

*I will focus on serving God;*
*He will take care of everything else.*

WEEK 17

## JOURNAL

*When planning a week, it is common to think of our to-do lists, but do we also consider the state of our souls? Take a moment to journal about your fears, joys, worries, desires, and stressors.*

## PRAYER

*Use the following prayer prompts to have a conversation with God about the week ahead.*

▶ **LORD, YOU ARE...**

▶ **LORD, I FEEL...**

▶ **LORD, HELP ME WITH...**

▶ **LORD, FORGIVE ME FOR...**

*Make a note of four or five people you are specifically praying for. It may be helpful to list their names in your planner so that you remember to pray for them throughout the week.*

○ _____

○ _____

○ _____

○ _____

○ _____

## SCRIPTURE MEDITATION

*For our struggle is not against flesh and blood,
but against the rulers, against the authorities,
against the cosmic powers of this darkness,
against evil, spiritual forces in the heavens.*
**EPHESIANS 6:12**

▶ *Reflect on what this verse tells you about who God is.*

▶ *Think about what this verse tells you about who you are.*

▶ *Write this verse in your planner, or put it in a place
where you will see it frequently. Throughout the week,
consider how it should affect the way you live.*

## GRATITUDE

*Reflect on the ways God has shown His faithfulness to you
over the last week. List five things you are thankful for.*

1. _____

2. _____

3. _____

4. _____

5. _____

### SPIRITUAL GROWTH | SERVE

*Who do you know that is in need? Think about what resources you have available to you (time, finances, prayer, etc.). Consider how you could serve those in need this week.*

### WEEK-AT-A-GLANCE CHECKLIST

*Whatever you do, do it from the heart, as something done for the Lord and not for people, knowing that you will receive the reward of an inheritance from the Lord. You serve the Lord Christ.*
*—Colossians 3:23-24*

○ **MAKE A PLAN FOR WHEN YOU WILL PRAY AND READ YOUR BIBLE THIS WEEK.**

○ **ADD ANY UPCOMING EVENTS TO YOUR CALENDAR.**

○ **JOT DOWN A TO-DO LIST OF TASKS THAT MUST BE COMPLETED THIS WEEK.**

○ **MAKE A NOTE OF YOUR TOP THREE PRIORITIES THIS WEEK TO STAY ON TRACK.**

### GOSPEL-CENTERED AFFIRMATION

*There is a spiritual battle happening in my life for which God equips me to fight.*

WEEK 18

### JOURNAL

*When planning a week, it is common to think of our to-do lists, but do we also consider the state of our souls? Take a moment to journal about your fears, joys, worries, desires, and stressors.*

### PRAYER

*Use the following prayer prompts to have a conversation with God about the week ahead.*

▶ **LORD, YOU ARE...**

▶ **LORD, I FEEL...**

▶ **LORD, HELP ME WITH...**

▶ **LORD, FORGIVE ME FOR...**

*Make a note of four or five people you are specifically praying for. It may be helpful to list their names in your planner so that you remember to pray for them throughout the week.*

○ _____

○ _____

○ _____

○ _____

○ _____

## SCRIPTURE MEDITATION

*So my word that comes from my mouth will
not return to me empty, but it will accomplish what
I please and will prosper in what I send it to do.*
**ISAIAH 55:11**

▶ *Reflect on what this verse tells you about who God is.*

▶ *Think about what this verse tells you about who you are.*

▶ *Write this verse in your planner, or put it in a place
where you will see it frequently. Throughout the week,
consider how it should affect the way you live.*

## GRATITUDE

*Reflect on the ways God has shown His faithfulness to you
over the last week. List five things you are thankful for.*

1. _____

2. _____

3. _____

4. _____

5. _____

## SPIRITUAL GROWTH | REST

*Think about what observing a Sabbath rest looks like to you.
Make a plan to intentionally rest this week.*

## WEEK-AT-A-GLANCE CHECKLIST

*Whatever you do, do it from the heart, as something done for
the Lord and not for people, knowing that you will receive the
reward of an inheritance from the Lord. You serve the Lord Christ.*
*—Colossians 3:23-24*

○ MAKE A PLAN FOR WHEN YOU WILL PRAY
AND READ YOUR BIBLE THIS WEEK.

○ ADD ANY UPCOMING EVENTS TO
YOUR CALENDAR.

○ JOT DOWN A TO-DO LIST OF TASKS THAT
MUST BE COMPLETED THIS WEEK.

○ MAKE A NOTE OF YOUR TOP THREE
PRIORITIES THIS WEEK TO STAY ON TRACK.

## GOSPEL-CENTERED AFFIRMATION

*God's Word never fails to accomplish His will.*

## JOURNAL

*When planning a week, it is common to think of our to-do lists, but do we also consider the state of our souls? Take a moment to journal about your fears, joys, worries, desires, and stressors.*

## PRAYER

*Use the following prayer prompts to have a conversation with God about the week ahead.*

▶ **LORD, YOU ARE...**

▶ **LORD, I FEEL...**

▶ **LORD, HELP ME WITH...**

▶ **LORD, FORGIVE ME FOR...**

*Make a note of four or five people you are specifically praying for. It may be helpful to list their names in your planner so that you remember to pray for them throughout the week.*

○ _____

○ _____

○ _____

○ _____

○ _____

## SCRIPTURE MEDITATION

*His divine power has given us everything required*
*for life and godliness through the knowledge of him*
*who called us by his own glory and goodness.*
**2 PETER 1:3**

▶ *Reflect on what this verse tells you about who God is.*

▶ *Think about what this verse tells you about who you are.*

▶ *Write this verse in your planner, or put it in a place*
   *where you will see it frequently. Throughout the week,*
   *consider how it should affect the way you live.*

## GRATITUDE

*Reflect on the ways God has shown His faithfulness to you*
*over the last week. List five things you are thankful for.*

1. _____

2. _____

3. _____

4. _____

5. _____

## SPIRITUAL GROWTH | FAST

*Consider fasting from something this week in order to focus on your need for God. What could you fast from? What would be the duration and frequency of your fast? Make a plan for how you will replace your fasted item with the pursuit of God and His Word.*

## WEEK-AT-A-GLANCE CHECKLIST

*Whatever you do, do it from the heart, as something done for the Lord and not for people, knowing that you will receive the reward of an inheritance from the Lord. You serve the Lord Christ.*
*— Colossians 3:23-24*

- ○ **MAKE A PLAN FOR WHEN YOU WILL PRAY AND READ YOUR BIBLE THIS WEEK.**

- ○ **ADD ANY UPCOMING EVENTS TO YOUR CALENDAR.**

- ○ **JOT DOWN A TO-DO LIST OF TASKS THAT MUST BE COMPLETED THIS WEEK.**

- ○ **MAKE A NOTE OF YOUR TOP THREE PRIORITIES THIS WEEK TO STAY ON TRACK.**

## GOSPEL-CENTERED AFFIRMATION

*In Christ, I have everything I need to live a godly life today and experience eternal life forevermore.*

### JOURNAL

*When planning a week, it is common to think of our to-do lists, but do we also consider the state of our souls? Take a moment to journal about your fears, joys, worries, desires, and stressors.*

### PRAYER

*Use the following prayer prompts to have a conversation with God about the week ahead.*

▶ **LORD, YOU ARE...**

▶ **LORD, I FEEL...**

▶ **LORD, HELP ME WITH...**

▶ **LORD, FORGIVE ME FOR...**

*Make a note of four or five people you are specifically praying for. It may be helpful to list their names in your planner so that you remember to pray for them throughout the week.*

○ _____

○ _____

○ _____

○ _____

○ _____

## SCRIPTURE MEDITATION

> *The Lord your God is among you,*
> *a warrior who saves. He will rejoice over*
> *you with gladness. He will be quiet in his*
> *love. He will delight in you with singing.*
> **ZEPHANIAH 3:17**

▶ *Reflect on what this verse tells you about who God is.*

▶ *Think about what this verse tells you about who you are.*

▶ *Write this verse in your planner, or put it in a place where you will see it frequently. Throughout the week, consider how it should affect the way you live.*

## GRATITUDE

*Reflect on the ways God has shown His faithfulness to you over the last week. List five things you are thankful for.*

1. _____

2. _____

3. _____

4. _____

5. _____

### SPIRITUAL GROWTH | FELLOWSHIP

*Plan a time to fellowship with friends this week. Go ahead and reach out to them now to get it on the calendar.*

### WEEK-AT-A-GLANCE CHECKLIST

*Whatever you do, do it from the heart, as something done for the Lord and not for people, knowing that you will receive the reward of an inheritance from the Lord. You serve the Lord Christ.*
—*Colossians 3:23-24*

○ MAKE A PLAN FOR WHEN YOU WILL PRAY AND READ YOUR BIBLE THIS WEEK.

○ ADD ANY UPCOMING EVENTS TO YOUR CALENDAR.

○ JOT DOWN A TO-DO LIST OF TASKS THAT MUST BE COMPLETED THIS WEEK.

○ MAKE A NOTE OF YOUR TOP THREE PRIORITIES THIS WEEK TO STAY ON TRACK.

### GOSPEL-CENTERED AFFIRMATION

*God is strong and tender,
a warrior and a loving Father.*

WEEK 21

### JOURNAL

*When planning a week, it is common to think of our to-do lists, but do we also consider the state of our souls? Take a moment to journal about your fears, joys, worries, desires, and stressors.*

### PRAYER

*Use the following prayer prompts to have a conversation with God about the week ahead.*

▶ **LORD, YOU ARE...**

▶ **LORD, I FEEL...**

▶ **LORD, HELP ME WITH...**

▶ **LORD, FORGIVE ME FOR...**

*Make a note of four or five people you are specifically praying for. It may be helpful to list their names in your planner so that you remember to pray for them throughout the week.*

○ _____

○ _____

○ _____

○ _____

○ _____

## SCRIPTURE MEDITATION

*See to it that no one repays evil for evil to anyone, but always pursue what is good for one another and for all.*

**1 THESSALONIANS 5:15**

▶ *Reflect on what this verse tells you about who God is.*

▶ *Think about what this verse tells you about who you are.*

▶ *Write this verse in your planner, or put it in a place where you will see it frequently. Throughout the week, consider how it should affect the way you live.*

## GRATITUDE

*Reflect on the ways God has shown His faithfulness to you over the last week. List five things you are thankful for.*

1. _____

2. _____

3. _____

4. _____

5. _____

## SPIRITUAL GROWTH | SERVE

*Who do you know that is in need? Think about what resources you have available to you (time, finances, prayer, etc.). Consider how you could serve those in need this week.*

## WEEK-AT-A-GLANCE CHECKLIST

*Whatever you do, do it from the heart, as something done for the Lord and not for people, knowing that you will receive the reward of an inheritance from the Lord. You serve the Lord Christ.*
*—Colossians 3:23-24*

- ○ **MAKE A PLAN FOR WHEN YOU WILL PRAY AND READ YOUR BIBLE THIS WEEK.**

- ○ **ADD ANY UPCOMING EVENTS TO YOUR CALENDAR.**

- ○ **JOT DOWN A TO-DO LIST OF TASKS THAT MUST BE COMPLETED THIS WEEK.**

- ○ **MAKE A NOTE OF YOUR TOP THREE PRIORITIES THIS WEEK TO STAY ON TRACK.**

## GOSPEL-CENTERED AFFIRMATION

*I choose to repay evil with good, knowing God deals with evil justly.*

WEEK 22

## JOURNAL

*When planning a week, it is common to think of our to-do lists, but do we also consider the state of our souls? Take a moment to journal about your fears, joys, worries, desires, and stressors.*

## PRAYER

*Use the following prayer prompts to have a conversation with God about the week ahead.*

▶ **LORD, YOU ARE...**

▶ **LORD, I FEEL...**

▶ **LORD, HELP ME WITH...**

▶ **LORD, FORGIVE ME FOR...**

*Make a note of four or five people you are specifically praying for. It may be helpful to list their names in your planner so that you remember to pray for them throughout the week.*

○ _____

○ _____

○ _____

○ _____

○ _____

## SCRIPTURE MEDITATION

*For whoever wants to save his life
will lose it, but whoever loses his life
because of me and the gospel will save it.*

**MARK 8:35**

▶ *Reflect on what this verse tells you about who God is.*

▶ *Think about what this verse tells you about who you are.*

▶ *Write this verse in your planner, or put it in a place
where you will see it frequently. Throughout the week,
consider how it should affect the way you live.*

## GRATITUDE

*Reflect on the ways God has shown His faithfulness to you
over the last week. List five things you are thankful for.*

1. _____

2. _____

3. _____

4. _____

5. _____

## SPIRITUAL GROWTH | REST

*Think about what observing a Sabbath rest looks like to you.*
*Make a plan to intentionally rest this week.*

## WEEK-AT-A-GLANCE CHECKLIST

*Whatever you do, do it from the heart, as something done for*
*the Lord and not for people, knowing that you will receive the*
*reward of an inheritance from the Lord. You serve the Lord Christ.*
*—Colossians 3:23-24*

○ **MAKE A PLAN FOR WHEN YOU WILL PRAY
AND READ YOUR BIBLE THIS WEEK.**

○ **ADD ANY UPCOMING EVENTS TO
YOUR CALENDAR.**

○ **JOT DOWN A TO-DO LIST OF TASKS THAT
MUST BE COMPLETED THIS WEEK.**

○ **MAKE A NOTE OF YOUR TOP THREE
PRIORITIES THIS WEEK TO STAY ON TRACK.**

## GOSPEL-CENTERED AFFIRMATION

*Living in a self-focused way leads to loss;*
*living in a Christ-focused way leads*
*to true and lasting life.*

## JOURNAL

*When planning a week, it is common to think of our to-do lists, but do we also consider the state of our souls? Take a moment to journal about your fears, joys, worries, desires, and stressors.*

## PRAYER

*Use the following prayer prompts to have a conversation with God about the week ahead.*

▶ LORD, YOU ARE...

▶ LORD, I FEEL...

▶ LORD, HELP ME WITH...

▶ LORD, FORGIVE ME FOR...

*Make a note of four or five people you are specifically praying for. It may be helpful to list their names in your planner so that you remember to pray for them throughout the week.*

○ _____

○ _____

○ _____

○ _____

○ _____

## SCRIPTURE MEDITATION

*When I am afraid, I will trust in you.*
**PSALM 56:3**

▶ *Reflect on what this verse tells you about who God is.*

▶ *Think about what this verse tells you about who you are.*

▶ *Write this verse in your planner, or put it in a place you will see it frequently. Throughout the week, consider how it should affect the way you live.*

## GRATITUDE

*Reflect on the ways God has shown His faithfulness to you over the last week. List five things you are thankful for.*

1. _____

2. _____

3. _____

4. _____

5. _____

## SPIRITUAL GROWTH | FAST

*Consider fasting from something this week in order to focus on your need for God. What could you fast from? What would be the duration and frequency of your fast? Make a plan for how you will replace your fasted item with the pursuit of God and His Word.*

## WEEK-AT-A-GLANCE CHECKLIST

*Whatever you do, do it from the heart, as something done for the Lord and not for people, knowing that you will receive the reward of an inheritance from the Lord. You serve the Lord Christ.*
*—Colossians 3:23-24*

- ○ MAKE A PLAN FOR WHEN YOU WILL PRAY AND READ YOUR BIBLE THIS WEEK.

- ○ ADD ANY UPCOMING EVENTS TO YOUR CALENDAR.

- ○ JOT DOWN A TO-DO LIST OF TASKS THAT MUST BE COMPLETED THIS WEEK.

- ○ MAKE A NOTE OF YOUR TOP THREE PRIORITIES THIS WEEK TO STAY ON TRACK.

## GOSPEL-CENTERED AFFIRMATION

*The trustworthiness of the Lord calms my fears.*

WEEK 24

## JOURNAL

*When planning a week, it is common to think of our to-do lists, but do we also consider the state of our souls? Take a moment to journal about your fears, joys, worries, desires, and stressors.*

## PRAYER

*Use the following prayer prompts to have a conversation with God about the week ahead.*

▶ **LORD, YOU ARE...**

▶ **LORD, I FEEL...**

▶ **LORD, HELP ME WITH...**

▶ **LORD, FORGIVE ME FOR...**

*Make a note of four or five people you are specifically praying for. It may be helpful to list their names in your planner so that you remember to pray for them throughout the week.*

○ _____

○ _____

○ _____

○ _____

○ _____

## SCRIPTURE MEDITATION

*When all has been heard, the conclusion
of the matter is this: fear God and keep his
commands, because this is for all humanity.*
**ECCLESIASTES 12:13**

▶ *Reflect on what this verse tells you about who God is.*

▶ *Think about what this verse tells you about who you are.*

▶ *Write this verse in your planner, or put it in a place
where you will see it frequently. Throughout the week,
consider how it should affect the way you live.*

## GRATITUDE

*Reflect on the ways God has shown His faithfulness to you
over the last week. List five things you are thankful for.*

1. _____

2. _____

3. _____

4. _____

5. _____

## SPIRITUAL GROWTH | FELLOWSHIP

*Plan a time to fellowship with friends this week. Go ahead and reach out to them now to get it on the calendar.*

## WEEK-AT-A-GLANCE CHECKLIST

*Whatever you do, do it from the heart, as something done for the Lord and not for people, knowing that you will receive the reward of an inheritance from the Lord. You serve the Lord Christ.*
—*Colossians 3:23-24*

○ **MAKE A PLAN FOR WHEN YOU WILL PRAY AND READ YOUR BIBLE THIS WEEK.**

○ **ADD ANY UPCOMING EVENTS TO YOUR CALENDAR.**

○ **JOT DOWN A TO-DO LIST OF TASKS THAT MUST BE COMPLETED THIS WEEK.**

○ **MAKE A NOTE OF YOUR TOP THREE PRIORITIES THIS WEEK TO STAY ON TRACK.**

## GOSPEL-CENTERED AFFIRMATION

*The purpose of my life is to glorify God and live in the way He instructs.*

## JOURNAL

*When planning a week, it is common to think of our to-do lists, but do we also consider the state of our souls? Take a moment to journal about your fears, joys, worries, desires, and stressors.*

## PRAYER

*Use the following prayer prompts to have a conversation with God about the week ahead.*

▶ **LORD, YOU ARE...**

▶ **LORD, I FEEL...**

▶ **LORD, HELP ME WITH...**

▶ **LORD, FORGIVE ME FOR...**

*Make a note of four or five people you are specifically praying for. It may be helpful to list their names in your planner so that you remember to pray for them throughout the week.*

○ _____

○ _____

○ _____

○ _____

○ _____

## SCRIPTURE MEDITATION

> *Who is a God like you, forgiving iniquity and passing over rebellion for the remnant of his inheritance? He does not hold on to his anger forever because he delights in faithful love.*
>
> **MICAH 7:18**

▶ *Reflect on what this verse tells you about who God is.*

▶ *Think about what this verse tells you about who you are.*

▶ *Write this verse in your planner, or put it in a place where you will see it frequently. Throughout the week, consider how it should affect the way you live.*

## GRATITUDE

*Reflect on the ways God has shown His faithfulness to you over the last week. List five things you are thankful for.*

1. _____

2. _____

3. _____

4. _____

5. _____

## SPIRITUAL GROWTH | SERVE

*Who do you know that is in need? Think about what resources you have available to you (time, finances, prayer, etc.). Consider how you could serve those in need this week.*

## WEEK-AT-A-GLANCE CHECKLIST

*Whatever you do, do it from the heart, as something done for the Lord and not for people, knowing that you will receive the reward of an inheritance from the Lord. You serve the Lord Christ.*
*—Colossians 3:23-24*

○ MAKE A PLAN FOR WHEN YOU WILL PRAY AND READ YOUR BIBLE THIS WEEK.

○ ADD ANY UPCOMING EVENTS TO YOUR CALENDAR.

○ JOT DOWN A TO-DO LIST OF TASKS THAT MUST BE COMPLETED THIS WEEK.

○ MAKE A NOTE OF YOUR TOP THREE PRIORITIES THIS WEEK TO STAY ON TRACK.

## GOSPEL-CENTERED AFFIRMATION

*No other love compares to God's faithful love.*

## JOURNAL

*When planning a week, it is common to think of our to-do lists, but do we also consider the state of our souls? Take a moment to journal about your fears, joys, worries, desires, and stressors.*

## PRAYER

*Use the following prayer prompts to have a conversation with God about the week ahead.*

▶ **LORD, YOU ARE...**

▶ **LORD, I FEEL...**

▶ **LORD, HELP ME WITH...**

▶ **LORD, FORGIVE ME FOR...**

*Make a note of four or five people you are specifically praying for. It may be helpful to list their names in your planner so that you remember to pray for them throughout the week.*

○ _____

○ _____

○ _____

○ _____

○ _____

## SCRIPTURE MEDITATION

*Jesus Christ is the same*
*yesterday, today, and forever.*
**HEBREWS 13:8**

▶ *Reflect on what this verse tells you about who God is.*

▶ *Think about what this verse tells you about who you are.*

▶ *Write this verse in your planner, or put it in a place*
*where you will see it frequently. Throughout the week,*
*consider how it should affect the way you live.*

## GRATITUDE

*Reflect on the ways God has shown His faithfulness to you*
*over the last week. List five things you are thankful for.*

1. _____

2. _____

3. _____

4. _____

5. _____

## SPIRITUAL GROWTH | REST

*Think about what observing a Sabbath rest looks like to you.*
*Make a plan to intentionally rest this week.*

## WEEK-AT-A-GLANCE CHECKLIST

*Whatever you do, do it from the heart, as something done for*
*the Lord and not for people, knowing that you will receive the*
*reward of an inheritance from the Lord. You serve the Lord Christ.*
*—Colossians 3:23-24*

- ○ MAKE A PLAN FOR WHEN YOU WILL PRAY
  AND READ YOUR BIBLE THIS WEEK.

- ○ ADD ANY UPCOMING EVENTS TO
  YOUR CALENDAR.

- ○ JOT DOWN A TO-DO LIST OF TASKS THAT
  MUST BE COMPLETED THIS WEEK.

- ○ MAKE A NOTE OF YOUR TOP THREE
  PRIORITIES THIS WEEK TO STAY ON TRACK.

## GOSPEL-CENTERED AFFIRMATION

*There is nothing and no one as reliable*
*as Jesus; He never changes.*

## JOURNAL

*When planning a week, it is common to think of our to-do lists, but do we also consider the state of our souls? Take a moment to journal about your fears, joys, worries, desires, and stressors.*

## PRAYER

*Use the following prayer prompts to have a conversation with God about the week ahead.*

▶ **LORD, YOU ARE...**

▶ **LORD, I FEEL...**

▶ **LORD, HELP ME WITH...**

▶ **LORD, FORGIVE ME FOR...**

*Make a note of four or five people you are specifically praying for. It may be helpful to list their names in your planner so that you remember to pray for them throughout the week.*

○ _____

○ _____

○ _____

○ _____

○ _____

## SCRIPTURE MEDITATION

*We demolish arguments and every proud thing that is raised up against the knowledge of God, and we take every thought captive to obey Christ.*
**2 CORINTHIANS 10:4B-5**

▶ *Reflect on what these verses tell you about who God is.*

▶ *Think about what these verses tell you about who you are.*

▶ *Write these verses in your planner, or put them in a place where you will see them frequently. Throughout the week, consider how they should affect the way you live.*

## GRATITUDE

*Reflect on the ways God has shown His faithfulness to you over the last week. List five things you are thankful for.*

1. _____

2. _____

3. _____

4. _____

5. _____

## SPIRITUAL GROWTH | FAST

*Consider fasting from something this week in order to focus on your need for God. What could you fast from? What would be the duration and frequency of your fast? Make a plan for how you will replace your fasted item with the pursuit of God and His Word.*

## WEEK-AT-A-GLANCE CHECKLIST

*Whatever you do, do it from the heart, as something done for the Lord and not for people, knowing that you will receive the reward of an inheritance from the Lord. You serve the Lord Christ.*
*— Colossians 3:23-24*

○ **MAKE A PLAN FOR WHEN YOU WILL PRAY AND READ YOUR BIBLE THIS WEEK.**

○ **ADD ANY UPCOMING EVENTS TO YOUR CALENDAR.**

○ **JOT DOWN A TO-DO LIST OF TASKS THAT MUST BE COMPLETED THIS WEEK.**

○ **MAKE A NOTE OF YOUR TOP THREE PRIORITIES THIS WEEK TO STAY ON TRACK.**

## GOSPEL-CENTERED AFFIRMATION

*With God's help, I can choose to think Christlike thoughts.*

## JOURNAL

*When planning a week, it is common to think of our to-do lists, but do we also consider the state of our souls? Take a moment to journal about your fears, joys, worries, desires, and stressors.*

## PRAYER

*Use the following prayer prompts to have a conversation with God about the week ahead.*

▶ **LORD, YOU ARE...**

▶ **LORD, I FEEL...**

▶ **LORD, HELP ME WITH...**

▶ **LORD, FORGIVE ME FOR...**

*Make a note of four or five people you are specifically praying for. It may be helpful to list their names in your planner so that you remember to pray for them throughout the week.*

○ _____

○ _____

○ _____

○ _____

○ _____

## SCRIPTURE MEDITATION

*Only goodness and faithful love will pursue me all the days of my life, and I will dwell in the house of the Lord as long as I live.*
**PSALM 23:6**

▶ *Reflect on what this verse tells you about who God is.*

▶ *Think about what this verse tells you about who you are.*

▶ *Write this verse in your planner, or put it in a place where you will see it frequently. Throughout the week, consider how it should affect the way you live.*

## GRATITUDE

*Reflect on the ways God has shown His faithfulness to you over the last week. List five things you are thankful for.*

1. _____

2. _____

3. _____

4. _____

5. _____

## SPIRITUAL GROWTH | FELLOWSHIP

*Plan a time to fellowship with friends this week. Go ahead and reach out to them now to get it on the calendar.*

## WEEK-AT-A-GLANCE CHECKLIST

*Whatever you do, do it from the heart, as something done for the Lord and not for people, knowing that you will receive the reward of an inheritance from the Lord. You serve the Lord Christ.*
*—Colossians 3:23-24*

○ **MAKE A PLAN FOR WHEN YOU WILL PRAY AND READ YOUR BIBLE THIS WEEK.**

○ **ADD ANY UPCOMING EVENTS TO YOUR CALENDAR.**

○ **JOT DOWN A TO-DO LIST OF TASKS THAT MUST BE COMPLETED THIS WEEK.**

○ **MAKE A NOTE OF YOUR TOP THREE PRIORITIES THIS WEEK TO STAY ON TRACK.**

## GOSPEL-CENTERED AFFIRMATION

*God's steadfast love pursues me all the days of my life.*

WEEK 29

## JOURNAL

*When planning a week, it is common to think of our to-do lists, but do we also consider the state of our souls? Take a moment to journal about your fears, joys, worries, desires, and stressors.*

## PRAYER

*Use the following prayer prompts to have a conversation with God about the week ahead.*

▶ **LORD, YOU ARE...**

▶ **LORD, I FEEL...**

▶ **LORD, HELP ME WITH...**

▶ **LORD, FORGIVE ME FOR...**

*Make a note of four or five people you are specifically praying for. It may be helpful to list their names in your planner so that you remember to pray for them throughout the week.*

○ _____

○ _____

○ _____

○ _____

○ _____

## SCRIPTURE MEDITATION

*Yet Lord, you are our Father;
we are the clay, and you are our potter;
we all are the work of your hands.*

**ISAIAH 64:8**

▶ *Reflect on what this verse tells you about who God is.*

▶ *Think about what this verse tells you about who you are.*

▶ *Write this verse in your planner, or put it in a place
where you will see it frequently. Throughout the week,
consider how it should affect the way you live.*

## GRATITUDE

*Reflect on the ways God has shown His faithfulness to you
over the last week. List five things you are thankful for.*

1. _____

2. _____

3. _____

4. _____

5. _____

## SPIRITUAL GROWTH | SERVE

*Who do you know that is in need? Think about what resources you have available to you (time, finances, prayer, etc.). Consider how you could serve those in need this week.*

## WEEK-AT-A-GLANCE CHECKLIST

*Whatever you do, do it from the heart, as something done for the Lord and not for people, knowing that you will receive the reward of an inheritance from the Lord. You serve the Lord Christ.*
*—Colossians 3:23-24*

- ○ **MAKE A PLAN FOR WHEN YOU WILL PRAY AND READ YOUR BIBLE THIS WEEK.**

- ○ **ADD ANY UPCOMING EVENTS TO YOUR CALENDAR.**

- ○ **JOT DOWN A TO-DO LIST OF TASKS THAT MUST BE COMPLETED THIS WEEK.**

- ○ **MAKE A NOTE OF YOUR TOP THREE PRIORITIES THIS WEEK TO STAY ON TRACK.**

## GOSPEL-CENTERED AFFIRMATION

*I am clay in the hand of God;*
*He shapes my life with fatherly care.*

WEEK 30

## JOURNAL

*When planning a week, it is common to think of our to-do lists, but do we also consider the state of our souls? Take a moment to journal about your fears, joys, worries, desires, and stressors.*

## PRAYER

*Use the following prayer prompts to have a conversation with God about the week ahead.*

▶ **LORD, YOU ARE...**

▶ **LORD, I FEEL...**

▶ **LORD, HELP ME WITH...**

▶ **LORD, FORGIVE ME FOR...**

*Make a note of four or five people you are specifically praying for. It may be helpful to list their names in your planner so that you remember to pray for them throughout the week.*

○ _____

○ _____

○ _____

○ _____

○ _____

## SCRIPTURE MEDITATION

> *Mankind, he has told each of you what is*
> *good and what it is the Lord requires of you:*
> *to act justly, to love faithfulness, and to*
> *walk humbly with your God.*
>
> **MICAH 6:8**

▶ *Reflect on what this verse tells you about who God is.*

▶ *Think about what this verse tells you about who you are.*

▶ *Write this verse in your planner, or put it in a place*
*where you will see it frequently. Throughout the week,*
*consider how it should affect the way you live.*

## GRATITUDE

*Reflect on the ways God has shown His faithfulness to you*
*over the last week. List five things you are thankful for.*

1. _____

2. _____

3. _____

4. _____

5. _____

## SPIRITUAL GROWTH | REST

*Think about what observing a Sabbath rest looks like to you.
Make a plan to intentionally rest this week.*

## WEEK-AT-A-GLANCE CHECKLIST

*Whatever you do, do it from the heart, as something done for
the Lord and not for people, knowing that you will receive the
reward of an inheritance from the Lord. You serve the Lord Christ.
—Colossians 3:23-24*

- ○ MAKE A PLAN FOR WHEN YOU WILL PRAY
  AND READ YOUR BIBLE THIS WEEK.

- ○ ADD ANY UPCOMING EVENTS TO
  YOUR CALENDAR.

- ○ JOT DOWN A TO-DO LIST OF TASKS THAT
  MUST BE COMPLETED THIS WEEK.

- ○ MAKE A NOTE OF YOUR TOP THREE
  PRIORITIES THIS WEEK TO STAY ON TRACK.

## GOSPEL-CENTERED AFFIRMATION

*It is good to act justly, love faithfulness,
and walk humbly with my God.*

## JOURNAL

*When planning a week, it is common to think of our to-do lists, but do we also consider the state of our souls? Take a moment to journal about your fears, joys, worries, desires, and stressors.*

## PRAYER

*Use the following prayer prompts to have a conversation with God about the week ahead.*

▶ **LORD, YOU ARE...**

▶ **LORD, I FEEL...**

▶ **LORD, HELP ME WITH...**

▶ **LORD, FORGIVE ME FOR...**

*Make a note of four or five people you are specifically praying for. It may be helpful to list their names in your planner so that you remember to pray for them throughout the week.*

○ _____

○ _____

○ _____

○ _____

○ _____

## SCRIPTURE MEDITATION

> *The Lord does not delay his promise,*
> *as some understand delay, but is patient*
> *with you, not wanting any to perish*
> *but all to come to repentance.*
>
> **2 PETER 3:9**

▶ *Reflect on what this verse tells you about who God is.*

▶ *Think about what this verse tells you about who you are.*

▶ *Write this verse in your planner, or put it in a place*
  *where you will see it frequently. Throughout the week,*
  *consider how it should affect the way you live.*

## GRATITUDE

*Reflect on the ways God has shown His faithfulness to you*
*over the last week. List five things you are thankful for.*

1. _____

2. _____

3. _____

4. _____

5. _____

## SPIRITUAL GROWTH | FAST

*Consider fasting from something this week in order to focus on your need for God. What could you fast from? What would be the duration and frequency of your fast? Make a plan for how you will replace your fasted item with the pursuit of God and His Word.*

## WEEK-AT-A-GLANCE CHECKLIST

*Whatever you do, do it from the heart, as something done for the Lord and not for people, knowing that you will receive the reward of an inheritance from the Lord. You serve the Lord Christ.*
*—Colossians 3:23-24*

- ○ **MAKE A PLAN FOR WHEN YOU WILL PRAY AND READ YOUR BIBLE THIS WEEK.**

- ○ **ADD ANY UPCOMING EVENTS TO YOUR CALENDAR.**

- ○ **JOT DOWN A TO-DO LIST OF TASKS THAT MUST BE COMPLETED THIS WEEK.**

- ○ **MAKE A NOTE OF YOUR TOP THREE PRIORITIES THIS WEEK TO STAY ON TRACK.**

## GOSPEL-CENTERED AFFIRMATION

*God's promises are not slow to arrive.*

## JOURNAL

*When planning a week, it is common to think of our to-do lists, but do we also consider the state of our souls? Take a moment to journal about your fears, joys, worries, desires, and stressors.*

## PRAYER

*Use the following prayer prompts to have a conversation with God about the week ahead.*

▶ **LORD, YOU ARE...**

▶ **LORD, I FEEL...**

▶ **LORD, HELP ME WITH...**

▶ **LORD, FORGIVE ME FOR...**

*Make a note of four or five people you are specifically praying for. It may be helpful to list their names in your planner so that you remember to pray for them throughout the week.*

○ _____

○ _____

○ _____

○ _____

○ _____

## SCRIPTURE MEDITATION

*Guard your heart above all else,*
*for it is the source of life.*
**PROVERBS 4:23**

▶ *Reflect on what this verse tells you about who God is.*

▶ *Think about what this verse tells you about who you are.*

▶ *Write this verse in your planner, or put it in a place*
*where you will see it frequently. Throughout the week,*
*consider how it should affect the way you live.*

## GRATITUDE

*Reflect on the ways God has shown His faithfulness to you*
*over the last week. List five things you are thankful for.*

1. _____

2. _____

3. _____

4. _____

5. _____

## SPIRITUAL GROWTH | FELLOWSHIP

*Plan a time to fellowship with friends this week. Go ahead and reach out to them now to get it on the calendar.*

## WEEK-AT-A-GLANCE CHECKLIST

*Whatever you do, do it from the heart, as something done for the Lord and not for people, knowing that you will receive the reward of an inheritance from the Lord. You serve the Lord Christ.*
*— Colossians 3:23-24*

○ MAKE A PLAN FOR WHEN YOU WILL PRAY
   AND READ YOUR BIBLE THIS WEEK.

○ ADD ANY UPCOMING EVENTS TO
   YOUR CALENDAR.

○ JOT DOWN A TO-DO LIST OF TASKS THAT
   MUST BE COMPLETED THIS WEEK.

○ MAKE A NOTE OF YOUR TOP THREE
   PRIORITIES THIS WEEK TO STAY ON TRACK.

## GOSPEL-CENTERED AFFIRMATION

*What I love determines the course of my life;*
*therefore, I choose to love the Lord.*

WEEK 33

## JOURNAL

*When planning a week, it is common to think of our to-do lists, but do we also consider the state of our souls? Take a moment to journal about your fears, joys, worries, desires, and stressors.*

## PRAYER

*Use the following prayer prompts to have a conversation with God about the week ahead.*

▶ **LORD, YOU ARE...**

▶ **LORD, I FEEL...**

▶ **LORD, HELP ME WITH...**

▶ **LORD, FORGIVE ME FOR...**

*Make a note of four or five people you are specifically praying for. It may be helpful to list their names in your planner so that you remember to pray for them throughout the week.*

○ _____

○ _____

○ _____

○ _____

○ _____

## SCRIPTURE MEDITATION

> *I heard every creature in heaven, on earth, under the earth, on the sea, and everything in them say, Blessing and honor and glory and power be to the one seated on the throne, and to the Lamb, forever and ever!*
> **REVELATION 5:13**

▶ *Reflect on what this verse tells you about who God is.*

▶ *Think about what this verse tells you about who you are.*

▶ *Write this verse in your planner, or put it in a place where you will see it frequently. Throughout the week, consider how it should affect the way you live.*

## GRATITUDE

*Reflect on the ways God has shown His faithfulness to you over the last week. List five things you are thankful for.*

1. _____

2. _____

3. _____

4. _____

5. _____

## SPIRITUAL GROWTH | SERVE

*Who do you know that is in need? Think about what resources you have available to you (time, finances, prayer, etc.). Consider how you could serve those in need this week.*

## WEEK-AT-A-GLANCE CHECKLIST

*Whatever you do, do it from the heart, as something done for the Lord and not for people, knowing that you will receive the reward of an inheritance from the Lord. You serve the Lord Christ.*
*— Colossians 3:23-24*

- ○ **MAKE A PLAN FOR WHEN YOU WILL PRAY AND READ YOUR BIBLE THIS WEEK.**

- ○ **ADD ANY UPCOMING EVENTS TO YOUR CALENDAR.**

- ○ **JOT DOWN A TO-DO LIST OF TASKS THAT MUST BE COMPLETED THIS WEEK.**

- ○ **MAKE A NOTE OF YOUR TOP THREE PRIORITIES THIS WEEK TO STAY ON TRACK.**

## GOSPEL-CENTERED AFFIRMATION

*One day, everyone and everything will worship the Lord.*

WEEK 34

## JOURNAL

*When planning a week, it is common to think of our to-do lists, but do we also consider the state of our souls? Take a moment to journal about your fears, joys, worries, desires, and stressors.*

## PRAYER

*Use the following prayer prompts to have a conversation with God about the week ahead.*

▶ **LORD, YOU ARE...**

▶ **LORD, I FEEL...**

▶ **LORD, HELP ME WITH...**

▶ **LORD, FORGIVE ME FOR...**

*Make a note of four or five people you are specifically praying for. It may be helpful to list their names in your planner so that you remember to pray for them throughout the week.*

○ _____

○ _____

○ _____

○ _____

○ _____

## SCRIPTURE MEDITATION

> *For the word of God is living and effective and sharper than any double-edged sword, penetrating as far as the separation of soul and spirit, joints and marrow. It is able to judge the thoughts and intentions of the heart.*
>
> **HEBREWS 4:12**

▶ *Reflect on what this verse tells you about who God is.*

▶ *Think about what this verse tells you about who you are.*

▶ *Write this verse in your planner, or put it in a place where you will see it frequently. Throughout the week, consider how it should affect the way you live.*

## GRATITUDE

*Reflect on the ways God has shown His faithfulness to you over the last week. List five things you are thankful for.*

1. _____

2. _____

3. _____

4. _____

5. _____

## SPIRITUAL GROWTH | REST

*Think about what observing a Sabbath rest looks like to you. Make a plan to intentionally rest this week.*

## WEEK-AT-A-GLANCE CHECKLIST

*Whatever you do, do it from the heart, as something done for the Lord and not for people, knowing that you will receive the reward of an inheritance from the Lord. You serve the Lord Christ.* —*Colossians 3:23-24*

- ○ MAKE A PLAN FOR WHEN YOU WILL PRAY AND READ YOUR BIBLE THIS WEEK.

- ○ ADD ANY UPCOMING EVENTS TO YOUR CALENDAR.

- ○ JOT DOWN A TO-DO LIST OF TASKS THAT MUST BE COMPLETED THIS WEEK.

- ○ MAKE A NOTE OF YOUR TOP THREE PRIORITIES THIS WEEK TO STAY ON TRACK.

## GOSPEL-CENTERED AFFIRMATION

*God can grant me the patience to be slow to anger.*

## JOURNAL

*When planning a week, it is common to think of our to-do lists, but do we also consider the state of our souls? Take a moment to journal about your fears, joys, worries, desires, and stressors.*

## PRAYER

*Use the following prayer prompts to have a conversation with God about the week ahead.*

▶ **LORD, YOU ARE...**

▶ **LORD, I FEEL...**

▶ **LORD, HELP ME WITH...**

▶ **LORD, FORGIVE ME FOR...**

*Make a note of four or five people you are specifically praying for. It may be helpful to list their names in your planner so that you remember to pray for them throughout the week.*

○ _____

○ _____

○ _____

○ _____

○ _____

## SCRIPTURE MEDITATION

*Don't let your spirit rush to be angry,
for anger abides in the heart of fools.*
**ECCLESIASTES 7:9**

▶ *Reflect on what this verse tells you about who God is.*

▶ *Think about what this verse tells you about who you are.*

▶ *Write this verse in your planner, or put it in a place
where you will see it frequently. Throughout the week,
consider how it should affect the way you live.*

## GRATITUDE

*Reflect on the ways God has shown His faithfulness to you
over the last week. List five things you are thankful for.*

1. _____

2. _____

3. _____

4. _____

5. _____

144

## SPIRITUAL GROWTH | FAST

*Consider fasting from something this week in order to focus on your need for God. What could you fast from? What would be the duration and frequency of your fast? Make a plan for how you will replace your fasted item with the pursuit of God and His Word.*

## WEEK-AT-A-GLANCE CHECKLIST

*Whatever you do, do it from the heart, as something done for the Lord and not for people, knowing that you will receive the reward of an inheritance from the Lord. You serve the Lord Christ.*
*—Colossians 3:23-24*

- ○ MAKE A PLAN FOR WHEN YOU WILL PRAY AND READ YOUR BIBLE THIS WEEK.

- ○ ADD ANY UPCOMING EVENTS TO YOUR CALENDAR.

- ○ JOT DOWN A TO-DO LIST OF TASKS THAT MUST BE COMPLETED THIS WEEK.

- ○ MAKE A NOTE OF YOUR TOP THREE PRIORITIES THIS WEEK TO STAY ON TRACK.

## GOSPEL-CENTERED AFFIRMATION

*I will not rush into anger but will act in wisdom.*

## JOURNAL

*When planning a week, it is common to think of our to-do lists, but do we also consider the state of our souls? Take a moment to journal about your fears, joys, worries, desires, and stressors.*

## PRAYER

*Use the following prayer prompts to have a conversation with God about the week ahead.*

▶ **LORD, YOU ARE...**

▶ **LORD, I FEEL...**

▶ **LORD, HELP ME WITH...**

▶ **LORD, FORGIVE ME FOR...**

*Make a note of four or five people you are specifically praying for. It may be helpful to list their names in your planner so that you remember to pray for them throughout the week.*

○ _____

○ _____

○ _____

○ _____

○ _____

## SCRIPTURE MEDITATION

*Love consists in this: not that we loved God,
but that he loved us and sent his Son to be
the atoning sacrifice for our sins.*

**1 JOHN 4:10**

▶ *Reflect on what this verse tells you about who God is.*

▶ *Think about what this verse tells you about who you are.*

▶ *Write this verse in your planner, or put it in a place
where you will see it frequently. Throughout the week,
consider how it should affect the way you live.*

## GRATITUDE

*Reflect on the ways God has shown His faithfulness to you
over the last week. List five things you are thankful for.*

1. _____

2. _____

3. _____

4. _____

5. _____

## SPIRITUAL GROWTH | FELLOWSHIP

*Plan a time to fellowship with friends this week. Go ahead and reach out to them now to get it on the calendar.*

## WEEK-AT-A-GLANCE CHECKLIST

*Whatever you do, do it from the heart, as something done for the Lord and not for people, knowing that you will receive the reward of an inheritance from the Lord. You serve the Lord Christ.*
*— Colossians 3:23-24*

- ○ MAKE A PLAN FOR WHEN YOU WILL PRAY AND READ YOUR BIBLE THIS WEEK.

- ○ ADD ANY UPCOMING EVENTS TO YOUR CALENDAR.

- ○ JOT DOWN A TO-DO LIST OF TASKS THAT MUST BE COMPLETED THIS WEEK.

- ○ MAKE A NOTE OF YOUR TOP THREE PRIORITIES THIS WEEK TO STAY ON TRACK.

## GOSPEL-CENTERED AFFIRMATION

*When I need to be assured of God's love, I need look no further than the sacrifice of Jesus.*

## JOURNAL

*When planning a week, it is common to think of our to-do lists, but do we also consider the state of our souls? Take a moment to journal about your fears, joys, worries, desires, and stressors.*

## PRAYER

*Use the following prayer prompts to have a conversation with God about the week ahead.*

▶ **LORD, YOU ARE...**

▶ **LORD, I FEEL...**

▶ **LORD, HELP ME WITH...**

▶ **LORD, FORGIVE ME FOR...**

*Make a note of four or five people you are specifically praying for. It may be helpful to list their names in your planner so that you remember to pray for them throughout the week.*

○ _____

○ _____

○ _____

○ _____

○ _____

## SCRIPTURE MEDITATION

*Trust in the Lord with all your heart, and do not rely on your own understanding; in all your ways know him, and he will make your paths straight.*

**PROVERBS 3:5-6**

▶ *Reflect on what this verse tells you about who God is.*

▶ *Think about what this verse tells you about who you are.*

▶ *Write this verse in your planner, or put it in a place where you will see it frequently. Throughout the week, consider how it should affect the way you live.*

## GRATITUDE

*Reflect on the ways God has shown His faithfulness to you over the last week. List five things you are thankful for.*

1. _____

2. _____

3. _____

4. _____

5. _____

## SPIRITUAL GROWTH | SERVE

*Who do you know that is in need? Think about what resources you have available to you (time, finances, prayer, etc.). Consider how you could serve those in need this week.*

## WEEK-AT-A-GLANCE CHECKLIST

*Whatever you do, do it from the heart, as something done for the Lord and not for people, knowing that you will receive the reward of an inheritance from the Lord. You serve the Lord Christ.*
*—Colossians 3:23-24*

- ○ **MAKE A PLAN FOR WHEN YOU WILL PRAY AND READ YOUR BIBLE THIS WEEK.**

- ○ **ADD ANY UPCOMING EVENTS TO YOUR CALENDAR.**

- ○ **JOT DOWN A TO-DO LIST OF TASKS THAT MUST BE COMPLETED THIS WEEK.**

- ○ **MAKE A NOTE OF YOUR TOP THREE PRIORITIES THIS WEEK TO STAY ON TRACK.**

## GOSPEL-CENTERED AFFIRMATION

*I entrust my whole life to the Lord.*

WEEK 38

## JOURNAL

*When planning a week, it is common to think of our to-do lists, but do we also consider the state of our souls? Take a moment to journal about your fears, joys, worries, desires, and stressors.*

## PRAYER

*Use the following prayer prompts to have a conversation with God about the week ahead.*

▶ **LORD, YOU ARE...**

▶ **LORD, I FEEL...**

▶ **LORD, HELP ME WITH...**

▶ **LORD, FORGIVE ME FOR...**

*Make a note of four or five people you are specifically praying for. It may be helpful to list their names in your planner so that you remember to pray for them throughout the week.*

○ _____

○ _____

○ _____

○ _____

○ _____

## SCRIPTURE MEDITATION

> *My help comes from the Lord,*
> *the Maker of heaven and earth.*
> **PSALM 121:2**

▶ *Reflect on what this verse tells you about who God is.*

▶ *Think about what this verse tells you about who you are.*

▶ *Write this verse in your planner, or put it in a place where you will see it frequently. Throughout the week, consider how it should affect the way you live.*

## GRATITUDE

*Reflect on the ways God has shown His faithfulness to you over the last week. List five things you are thankful for.*

1. _____

2. _____

3. _____

4. _____

5. _____

## SPIRITUAL GROWTH | REST

*Think about what observing a Sabbath rest looks like to you. Make a plan to intentionally rest this week.*

## WEEK-AT-A-GLANCE CHECKLIST

*Whatever you do, do it from the heart, as something done for the Lord and not for people, knowing that you will receive the reward of an inheritance from the Lord. You serve the Lord Christ.*
*—Colossians 3:23-24*

- ○ **MAKE A PLAN FOR WHEN YOU WILL PRAY AND READ YOUR BIBLE THIS WEEK.**

- ○ **ADD ANY UPCOMING EVENTS TO YOUR CALENDAR.**

- ○ **JOT DOWN A TO-DO LIST OF TASKS THAT MUST BE COMPLETED THIS WEEK.**

- ○ **MAKE A NOTE OF YOUR TOP THREE PRIORITIES THIS WEEK TO STAY ON TRACK.**

## GOSPEL-CENTERED AFFIRMATION

*The Creator of the whole world is the One who helps me.*

## JOURNAL

*When planning a week, it is common to think of our to-do lists, but do we also consider the state of our souls? Take a moment to journal about your fears, joys, worries, desires, and stressors.*

## PRAYER

*Use the following prayer prompts to have a conversation with God about the week ahead.*

▶ **LORD, YOU ARE...**

▶ **LORD, I FEEL...**

▶ **LORD, HELP ME WITH...**

▶ **LORD, FORGIVE ME FOR...**

*Make a note of four or five people you are specifically praying for. It may be helpful to list their names in your planner so that you remember to pray for them throughout the week.*

○ _____

○ _____

○ _____

○ _____

○ _____

## SCRIPTURE MEDITATION

*Be alert, stand firm in the faith,*
*be courageous, be strong.*
**1 CORINTHIANS 16:13**

▶ *Reflect on what this verse tells you about who God is.*

▶ *Think about what this verse tells you about who you are.*

▶ *Write this verse in your planner, or put it in a place where you will see it frequently. Throughout the week, consider how it should affect the way you live.*

## GRATITUDE

*Reflect on the ways God has shown His faithfulness to you over the last week. List five things you are thankful for.*

1. _____

2. _____

3. _____

4. _____

5. _____

## SPIRITUAL GROWTH | FAST

*Consider fasting from something this week in order to focus on your need for God. What could you fast from? What would be the duration and frequency of your fast? Make a plan for how you will replace your fasted item with the pursuit of God and His Word.*

## WEEK-AT-A-GLANCE CHECKLIST

*Whatever you do, do it from the heart, as something done for the Lord and not for people, knowing that you will receive the reward of an inheritance from the Lord. You serve the Lord Christ.*
*—Colossians 3:23-24*

- ○ MAKE A PLAN FOR WHEN YOU WILL PRAY AND READ YOUR BIBLE THIS WEEK.

- ○ ADD ANY UPCOMING EVENTS TO YOUR CALENDAR.

- ○ JOT DOWN A TO-DO LIST OF TASKS THAT MUST BE COMPLETED THIS WEEK.

- ○ MAKE A NOTE OF YOUR TOP THREE PRIORITIES THIS WEEK TO STAY ON TRACK.

## GOSPEL-CENTERED AFFIRMATION

*I will stand strong in the truth of Scripture rather than being swept away by every whim.*

WEEK 40

## JOURNAL

*When planning a week, it is common to think of our to-do lists, but do we also consider the state of our souls? Take a moment to journal about your fears, joys, worries, desires, and stressors.*

## PRAYER

*Use the following prayer prompts to have a conversation with God about the week ahead.*

▶ **LORD, YOU ARE...**

▶ **LORD, I FEEL...**

▶ **LORD, HELP ME WITH...**

▶ **LORD, FORGIVE ME FOR...**

*Make a note of four or five people you are specifically praying for. It may be helpful to list their names in your planner so that you remember to pray for them throughout the week.*

○ _____

○ _____

○ _____

○ _____

○ _____

## SCRIPTURE MEDITATION

*The grass withers, the flowers fade,*
*but the word of our God remains forever.*
**ISAIAH 40:8**

▶ *Reflect on what this verse tells you about who God is.*

▶ *Think about what this verse tells you about who you are.*

▶ *Write this verse in your planner, or put it in a place*
   *where you will see it frequently. Throughout the week,*
   *consider how it should affect the way you live.*

## GRATITUDE

*Reflect on the ways God has shown His faithfulness to you*
*over the last week. List five things you are thankful for.*

1. _____

2. _____

3. _____

4. _____

5. _____

## SPIRITUAL GROWTH | FELLOWSHIP

*Plan a time to fellowship with friends this week. Go ahead and reach out to them now to get it on the calendar.*

## WEEK-AT-A-GLANCE CHECKLIST

*Whatever you do, do it from the heart, as something done for the Lord and not for people, knowing that you will receive the reward of an inheritance from the Lord. You serve the Lord Christ.*
*— Colossians 3:23-24*

○ MAKE A PLAN FOR WHEN YOU WILL PRAY AND READ YOUR BIBLE THIS WEEK.

○ ADD ANY UPCOMING EVENTS TO YOUR CALENDAR.

○ JOT DOWN A TO-DO LIST OF TASKS THAT MUST BE COMPLETED THIS WEEK.

○ MAKE A NOTE OF YOUR TOP THREE PRIORITIES THIS WEEK TO STAY ON TRACK.

## GOSPEL-CENTERED AFFIRMATION

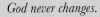

*God never changes.*

## JOURNAL

*When planning a week, it is common to think of our to-do lists, but do we also consider the state of our souls? Take a moment to journal about your fears, joys, worries, desires, and stressors.*

## PRAYER

*Use the following prayer prompts to have a conversation with God about the week ahead.*

▶ **LORD, YOU ARE...**

▶ **LORD, I FEEL...**

▶ **LORD, HELP ME WITH...**

▶ **LORD, FORGIVE ME FOR...**

*Make a note of four or five people you are specifically praying for. It may be helpful to list their names in your planner so that you remember to pray for them throughout the week.*

○  _____

○  _____

○  _____

○  _____

○  _____

## SCRIPTURE MEDITATION

*When I am filled with cares,*
*your comfort brings me joy.*
**PSALM 94:19**

▶ *Reflect on what this verse tells you about who God is.*

▶ *Think about what this verse tells you about who you are.*

▶ *Write this verse in your planner, or put it in a place
where you will see it frequently. Throughout the week,
consider how it should affect the way you live.*

## GRATITUDE

*Reflect on the ways God has shown His faithfulness to you
over the last week. List five things you are thankful for.*

1. _____

2. _____

3. _____

4. _____

5. _____

## SPIRITUAL GROWTH | SERVE

*Who do you know that is in need? Think about what resources you have available to you (time, finances, prayer, etc.). Consider how you could serve those in need this week.*

## WEEK-AT-A-GLANCE CHECKLIST

*Whatever you do, do it from the heart, as something done for the Lord and not for people, knowing that you will receive the reward of an inheritance from the Lord. You serve the Lord Christ.*
*— Colossians 3:23-24*

○ MAKE A PLAN FOR WHEN YOU WILL PRAY AND READ YOUR BIBLE THIS WEEK.

○ ADD ANY UPCOMING EVENTS TO YOUR CALENDAR.

○ JOT DOWN A TO-DO LIST OF TASKS THAT MUST BE COMPLETED THIS WEEK.

○ MAKE A NOTE OF YOUR TOP THREE PRIORITIES THIS WEEK TO STAY ON TRACK.

## GOSPEL-CENTERED AFFIRMATION

*Even when I am overcome with concerns, I find joy in the nearness of God.*

WEEK 42

## JOURNAL

*When planning a week, it is common to think of our to-do lists, but do we also consider the state of our souls? Take a moment to journal about your fears, joys, worries, desires, and stressors.*

## PRAYER

*Use the following prayer prompts to have a conversation with God about the week ahead.*

▷ **LORD, YOU ARE...**

▷ **LORD, I FEEL...**

▷ **LORD, HELP ME WITH...**

▷ **LORD, FORGIVE ME FOR...**

*Make a note of four or five people you are specifically praying for. It may be helpful to list their names in your planner so that you remember to pray for them throughout the week.*

○ _____

○ _____

○ _____

○ _____

○ _____

## SCRIPTURE MEDITATION

*But love your enemies, do what is good, and lend, expecting nothing in return. Then your reward will be great, and you will be children of the Most High. For he is gracious to the ungrateful and evil.*

**LUKE 6:35**

▶ *Reflect on what this verse tells you about who God is.*

▶ *Think about what this verse tells you about who you are.*

▶ *Write this verse in your planner, or put it in a place you will see it frequently. Throughout the week, consider how it should affect the way you live.*

## GRATITUDE

*Reflect on the ways God has shown His faithfulness to you over the last week. List five things you are thankful for.*

1. _____

2. _____

3. _____

4. _____

5. _____

## SPIRITUAL GROWTH | REST

*Think about what observing a Sabbath rest looks like to you.*
*Make a plan to intentionally rest this week.*

## WEEK-AT-A-GLANCE CHECKLIST

*Whatever you do, do it from the heart, as something done for*
*the Lord and not for people, knowing that you will receive the*
*reward of an inheritance from the Lord. You serve the Lord Christ.*
*—Colossians 3:23-24*

- ○ **MAKE A PLAN FOR WHEN YOU WILL PRAY AND READ YOUR BIBLE THIS WEEK.**

- ○ **ADD ANY UPCOMING EVENTS TO YOUR CALENDAR.**

- ○ **JOT DOWN A TO-DO LIST OF TASKS THAT MUST BE COMPLETED THIS WEEK.**

- ○ **MAKE A NOTE OF YOUR TOP THREE PRIORITIES THIS WEEK TO STAY ON TRACK.**

## GOSPEL-CENTERED AFFIRMATION

*God rewards those who show*
*undeserved grace to others.*

WEEK 43

## JOURNAL

*When planning a week, it is common to think of our to-do lists, but do we also consider the state of our souls? Take a moment to journal about your fears, joys, worries, desires, and stressors.*

## PRAYER

*Use the following prayer prompts to have a conversation with God about the week ahead.*

▶ **LORD, YOU ARE...**

▶ **LORD, I FEEL...**

▶ **LORD, HELP ME WITH...**

▶ **LORD, FORGIVE ME FOR...**

*Make a note of four or five people you are specifically praying for. It may be helpful to list their names in your planner so that you remember to pray for them throughout the week.*

○ _____

○ _____

○ _____

○ _____

○ _____

## SCRIPTURE MEDITATION

> *But I will sing of your strength and*
> *will joyfully proclaim your faithful love*
> *in the morning. For you have been a stronghold*
> *for me, a refuge in my day of trouble.*
> **PSALM 59:16**

▶ *Reflect on what this verse tells you about who God is.*

▶ *Think about what this verse tells you about who you are.*

▶ *Write this verse in your planner, or put it in a place*
*where you will see it frequently. Throughout the week,*
*consider how it should affect the way you live..*

## GRATITUDE

*Reflect on the ways God has shown His faithfulness to you*
*over the last week. List five things you are thankful for.*

1. _____

2. _____

3. _____

4. _____

5. _____

## SPIRITUAL GROWTH | FAST

*Consider fasting from something this week in order to focus on your need for God. What could you fast from? What would be the duration and frequency of your fast? Make a plan for how you will replace your fasted item with the pursuit of God and His Word.*

## WEEK-AT-A-GLANCE CHECKLIST

*Whatever you do, do it from the heart, as something done for the Lord and not for people, knowing that you will receive the reward of an inheritance from the Lord. You serve the Lord Christ.*
*—Colossians 3:23-24*

- ○ **MAKE A PLAN FOR WHEN YOU WILL PRAY AND READ YOUR BIBLE THIS WEEK.**

- ○ **ADD ANY UPCOMING EVENTS TO YOUR CALENDAR.**

- ○ **JOT DOWN A TO-DO LIST OF TASKS THAT MUST BE COMPLETED THIS WEEK.**

- ○ **MAKE A NOTE OF YOUR TOP THREE PRIORITIES THIS WEEK TO STAY ON TRACK.**

## GOSPEL-CENTERED AFFIRMATION

*The Lord is my strength and refuge.*

## JOURNAL

*When planning a week, it is common to think of our to-do lists, but do we also consider the state of our souls? Take a moment to journal about your fears, joys, worries, desires, and stressors.*

## PRAYER

*Use the following prayer prompts to have a conversation with God about the week ahead.*

▶ **LORD, YOU ARE...**

▶ **LORD, I FEEL...**

▶ **LORD, HELP ME WITH...**

▶ **LORD, FORGIVE ME FOR...**

*Make a note of four or five people you are specifically praying for. It may be helpful to list their names in your planner so that you remember to pray for them throughout the week.*

○ _____

○ _____

○ _____

○ _____

○ _____

## SCRIPTURE MEDITATION

*Jesus said to him, "'If you can'? Everything is possible for the one who believes."*
**MARK 9:23**

▶ *Reflect on what this verse tells you about who God is.*

▶ *Think about what this verse tells you about who you are.*

▶ *Write this verse in your planner, or put it in a place where you will see it frequently. Throughout the week, consider how it should affect the way you live.*

## GRATITUDE

*Reflect on the ways God has shown His faithfulness to you over the last week. List five things you are thankful for.*

1. _____

2. _____

3. _____

4. _____

5. _____

## SPIRITUAL GROWTH | FELLOWSHIP

*Plan a time to fellowship with friends this week. Go ahead and reach out to them now to get it on the calendar.*

## WEEK-AT-A-GLANCE CHECKLIST

*Whatever you do, do it from the heart, as something done for the Lord and not for people, knowing that you will receive the reward of an inheritance from the Lord. You serve the Lord Christ.*
*—Colossians 3:23-24*

○ MAKE A PLAN FOR WHEN YOU WILL PRAY AND READ YOUR BIBLE THIS WEEK.

○ ADD ANY UPCOMING EVENTS TO YOUR CALENDAR.

○ JOT DOWN A TO-DO LIST OF TASKS THAT MUST BE COMPLETED THIS WEEK.

○ MAKE A NOTE OF YOUR TOP THREE PRIORITIES THIS WEEK TO STAY ON TRACK.

## GOSPEL-CENTERED AFFIRMATION

*I believe that anything is possible for the Lord.*

WEEK 45

## JOURNAL

*When planning a week, it is common to think of our to-do lists, but do we also consider the state of our souls? Take a moment to journal about your fears, joys, worries, desires, and stressors.*

## PRAYER

*Use the following prayer prompts to have a conversation with God about the week ahead.*

▶ LORD, YOU ARE...

▶ LORD, I FEEL...

▶ LORD, HELP ME WITH...

▶ LORD, FORGIVE ME FOR...

*Make a note of four or five people you are specifically praying for. It may be helpful to list their names in your planner so that you remember to pray for them throughout the week.*

○ _____

○ _____

○ _____

○ _____

○ _____

## SCRIPTURE MEDITATION

*Therefore, brothers and sisters, in view of the mercies of God, I urge you to present your bodies as a living sacrifice, holy and pleasing to God; this is your true worship.*

**ROMANS 12:1**

▶ *Reflect on what this verse tells you about who God is.*

▶ *Think about what this verse tells you about who you are.*

▶ *Write this verse in your planner, or put it in a place where you will see it frequently. Throughout the week, consider how it should affect the way you live.*

## GRATITUDE

*Reflect on the ways God has shown His faithfulness to you over the last week. List five things you are thankful for.*

1. _____

2. _____

3. _____

4. _____

5. _____

## SPIRITUAL GROWTH | SERVE

*Who do you know that is in need? Think about what resources you have available to you (time, finances, prayer, etc.). Consider how you could serve those in need this week.*

## WEEK-AT-A-GLANCE CHECKLIST

*Whatever you do, do it from the heart, as something done for the Lord and not for people, knowing that you will receive the reward of an inheritance from the Lord. You serve the Lord Christ.*
*—Colossians 3:23-24*

- ○ MAKE A PLAN FOR WHEN YOU WILL PRAY AND READ YOUR BIBLE THIS WEEK.

- ○ ADD ANY UPCOMING EVENTS TO YOUR CALENDAR.

- ○ JOT DOWN A TO-DO LIST OF TASKS THAT MUST BE COMPLETED THIS WEEK.

- ○ MAKE A NOTE OF YOUR TOP THREE PRIORITIES THIS WEEK TO STAY ON TRACK.

## GOSPEL-CENTERED AFFIRMATION

*May my speech and actions be an act of worship to the Lord.*

WEEK 46

## JOURNAL

*When planning a week, it is common to think of our to-do lists, but do we also consider the state of our souls? Take a moment to journal about your fears, joys, worries, desires, and stressors.*

## PRAYER

*Use the following prayer prompts to have a conversation with God about the week ahead.*

▶ **LORD, YOU ARE...**

▶ **LORD, I FEEL...**

▶ **LORD, HELP ME WITH...**

▶ **LORD, FORGIVE ME FOR...**

*Make a note of four or five people you are specifically praying for. It may be helpful to list their names in your planner so that you remember to pray for them throughout the week.*

○ _____

○ _____

○ _____

○ _____

○ _____

## SCRIPTURE MEDITATION

*Give thanks to the Lord, for he is good;*
*his faithful love endures forever.*
**1 CHRONICLES 16:34**

▶ *Reflect on what this verse tells you about who God is.*

▶ *Think about what this verse tells you about who you are.*

▶ *Write this verse in your planner, or put it in a place*
*where you will see it frequently. Throughout the week,*
*consider how it should affect the way you live.*

## GRATITUDE

*Reflect on the ways God has shown His faithfulness to you*
*over the last week. List five things you are thankful for.*

1. _____

2. _____

3. _____

4. _____

5. _____

## SPIRITUAL GROWTH | REST

*Think about what observing a Sabbath rest looks like to you.*
*Make a plan to intentionally rest this week.*

## WEEK-AT-A-GLANCE CHECKLIST

*Whatever you do, do it from the heart, as something done for*
*the Lord and not for people, knowing that you will receive the*
*reward of an inheritance from the Lord. You serve the Lord Christ.*
*—Colossians 3:23-24*

- ○ **MAKE A PLAN FOR WHEN YOU WILL PRAY AND READ YOUR BIBLE THIS WEEK.**

- ○ **ADD ANY UPCOMING EVENTS TO YOUR CALENDAR.**

- ○ **JOT DOWN A TO-DO LIST OF TASKS THAT MUST BE COMPLETED THIS WEEK.**

- ○ **MAKE A NOTE OF YOUR TOP THREE PRIORITIES THIS WEEK TO STAY ON TRACK.**

## GOSPEL-CENTERED AFFIRMATION

*God has steadfast love for me.*

WEEK 47

## JOURNAL

*When planning a week, it is common to think of our to-do lists, but do we also consider the state of our souls? Take a moment to journal about your fears, joys, worries, desires, and stressors.*

## PRAYER

*Use the following prayer prompts to have a conversation with God about the week ahead.*

▷ **LORD, YOU ARE...**

▷ **LORD, I FEEL...**

▷ **LORD, HELP ME WITH...**

▷ **LORD, FORGIVE ME FOR...**

*Make a note of four or five people you are specifically praying for. It may be helpful to list their names in your planner so that you remember to pray for them throughout the week.*

○ _____

○ _____

○ _____

○ _____

○ _____

## SCRIPTURE MEDITATION

*Love one another deeply as brothers and sisters.*
*Outdo one another in showing honor.*
**ROMANS 12:10**

▶ *Reflect on what this verse tells you about who God is.*

▶ *Think about what this verse tells you about who you are.*

▶ *Write this verse in your planner, or put it in a place where you will see it frequently. Throughout the week, consider how it should affect the way you live.*

## GRATITUDE

*Reflect on the ways God has shown His faithfulness to you over the last week. List five things you are thankful for.*

1. _____

2. _____

3. _____

4. _____

5. _____

## SPIRITUAL GROWTH | FAST

*Consider fasting from something this week in order to focus on your need for God. What could you fast from? What would be the duration and frequency of your fast? Make a plan for how you will replace your fasted item with the pursuit of God and His Word.*

## WEEK-AT-A-GLANCE CHECKLIST

*Whatever you do, do it from the heart, as something done for the Lord and not for people, knowing that you will receive the reward of an inheritance from the Lord. You serve the Lord Christ.*
*—Colossians 3:23-24*

○ **MAKE A PLAN FOR WHEN YOU WILL PRAY AND READ YOUR BIBLE THIS WEEK.**

○ **ADD ANY UPCOMING EVENTS TO YOUR CALENDAR.**

○ **JOT DOWN A TO-DO LIST OF TASKS THAT MUST BE COMPLETED THIS WEEK.**

○ **MAKE A NOTE OF YOUR TOP THREE PRIORITIES THIS WEEK TO STAY ON TRACK.**

## GOSPEL-CENTERED AFFIRMATION

*I will seek to serve and honor others first.*

## JOURNAL

*When planning a week, it is common to think of our to-do lists, but do we also consider the state of our souls? Take a moment to journal about your fears, joys, worries, desires, and stressors.*

## PRAYER

*Use the following prayer prompts to have a conversation with God about the week ahead.*

▶ LORD, YOU ARE...

▶ LORD, I FEEL...

▶ LORD, HELP ME WITH...

▶ LORD, FORGIVE ME FOR...

*Make a note of four or five people you are specifically praying for. It may be helpful to list their names in your planner so that you remember to pray for them throughout the week.*

○ _____

○ _____

○ _____

○ _____

○ _____

## SCRIPTURE MEDITATION

> *For we are his workmanship, created in Christ Jesus for good works, which God prepared ahead of time for us to do.*
> **EPHESIANS 2:10**

▶ *Reflect on what this verse tells you about who God is.*

▶ *Think about what this verse tells you about who you are.*

▶ *Write this verse in your planner, or put it in a place where you will see it frequently. Throughout the week, consider how it should affect the way you live.*

## GRATITUDE

*Reflect on the ways God has shown His faithfulness to you over the last week. List five things you are thankful for.*

1. _____

2. _____

3. _____

4. _____

5. _____

## SPIRITUAL GROWTH | FELLOWSHIP

*Plan a time to fellowship with friends this week. Go ahead and reach out to them now to get it on the calendar.*

## WEEK-AT-A-GLANCE CHECKLIST

*Whatever you do, do it from the heart, as something done for the Lord and not for people, knowing that you will receive the reward of an inheritance from the Lord. You serve the Lord Christ.* —*Colossians 3:23-24*

- ○ **MAKE A PLAN FOR WHEN YOU WILL PRAY AND READ YOUR BIBLE THIS WEEK.**

- ○ **ADD ANY UPCOMING EVENTS TO YOUR CALENDAR.**

- ○ **JOT DOWN A TO-DO LIST OF TASKS THAT MUST BE COMPLETED THIS WEEK.**

- ○ **MAKE A NOTE OF YOUR TOP THREE PRIORITIES THIS WEEK TO STAY ON TRACK.**

## GOSPEL-CENTERED AFFIRMATION

*God has planned good works for me to do.*

WEEK 49

## JOURNAL

*When planning a week, it is common to think of our to-do lists, but do we also consider the state of our souls? Take a moment to journal about your fears, joys, worries, desires, and stressors.*

## PRAYER

*Use the following prayer prompts to have a conversation with God about the week ahead.*

▶ **LORD, YOU ARE...**

▶ **LORD, I FEEL...**

▶ **LORD, HELP ME WITH...**

▶ **LORD, FORGIVE ME FOR...**

*Make a note of four or five people you are specifically praying for. It may be helpful to list their names in your planner so that you remember to pray for them throughout the week.*

○ _____

○ _____

○ _____

○ _____

○ _____

## SCRIPTURE MEDITATION

*Now to him who is able to do above and beyond all that we ask or think according to the power that works in us—to him be the glory in the church and in Christ Jesus to all generations, forever and ever. Amen.*
**EPHESIANS 3:20-21**

▶ *Reflect on what these verses tell you about who God is.*

▶ *Think about what these verses tell you about who you are.*

▶ *Write these verses in your planner, or put them in a place you will see them frequently. Throughout the week, consider how these verses should affect the way you live.*

## GRATITUDE

*Reflect on the ways God has shown His faithfulness to you over the last week. List five things you are thankful for.*

1. _____

2. _____

3. _____

4. _____

5. _____

## SPIRITUAL GROWTH | SERVE

*Who do you know that is in need? Think about what resources you have available to you (time, finances, prayer, etc.). Consider how you could serve those in need this week.*

## WEEK-AT-A-GLANCE CHECKLIST

*Whatever you do, do it from the heart, as something done for the Lord and not for people, knowing that you will receive the reward of an inheritance from the Lord. You serve the Lord Christ.*
*—Colossians 3:23-24*

- ○ **MAKE A PLAN FOR WHEN YOU WILL PRAY AND READ YOUR BIBLE THIS WEEK.**

- ○ **ADD ANY UPCOMING EVENTS TO YOUR CALENDAR.**

- ○ **JOT DOWN A TO-DO LIST OF TASKS THAT MUST BE COMPLETED THIS WEEK.**

- ○ **MAKE A NOTE OF YOUR TOP THREE PRIORITIES THIS WEEK TO STAY ON TRACK.**

## GOSPEL-CENTERED AFFIRMATION

*God works powerfully in me.*

## JOURNAL

*When planning a week, it is common to think of our to-do lists, but do we also consider the state of our souls? Take a moment to journal about your fears, joys, worries, desires, and stressors.*

## PRAYER

*Use the following prayer prompts to have a conversation with God about the week ahead.*

▶ **LORD, YOU ARE...**

▶ **LORD, I FEEL...**

▶ **LORD, HELP ME WITH...**

▶ **LORD, FORGIVE ME FOR...**

*Make a note of four or five people you are specifically praying for. It may be helpful to list their names in your planner so that you remember to pray for them throughout the week.*

○ _____

○ _____

○ _____

○ _____

○ _____

## SCRIPTURE MEDITATION

> *"Don't let your heart be troubled.*
> *Believe in God; believe also in me."*
> **JOHN 14:1**

▶ *Reflect on what this verse tells you about who God is.*

▶ *Think about what this verse tells you about who you are.*

▶ *Write this verse in your planner, or put it in a place you will see it frequently. Throughout the week, consider how it should affect the way you live.*

## GRATITUDE

*Reflect on the ways God has shown His faithfulness to you over the last week. List five things you are thankful for.*

1. _____

2. _____

3. _____

4. _____

5. _____

## SPIRITUAL GROWTH | REST

*Think about what observing a Sabbath rest looks like to you.*
*Make a plan to intentionally rest this week.*

## WEEK-AT-A-GLANCE CHECKLIST

*Whatever you do, do it from the heart, as something done for*
*the Lord and not for people, knowing that you will receive the*
*reward of an inheritance from the Lord. You serve the Lord Christ.*
*—Colossians 3:23-24*

○ MAKE A PLAN FOR WHEN YOU WILL PRAY
  AND READ YOUR BIBLE THIS WEEK.

○ ADD ANY UPCOMING EVENTS TO
  YOUR CALENDAR.

○ JOT DOWN A TO-DO LIST OF TASKS THAT
  MUST BE COMPLETED THIS WEEK.

○ MAKE A NOTE OF YOUR TOP THREE
  PRIORITIES THIS WEEK TO STAY ON TRACK.

## GOSPEL-CENTERED AFFIRMATION

*When my heart is troubled, I will trust in God.*

## JOURNAL

*When planning a week, it is common to think of our to-do lists, but do we also consider the state of our souls? Take a moment to journal about your fears, joys, worries, desires, and stressors.*

## PRAYER

*Use the following prayer prompts to have a conversation with God about the week ahead.*

▶ **LORD, YOU ARE...**

▶ **LORD, I FEEL...**

▶ **LORD, HELP ME WITH...**

▶ **LORD, FORGIVE ME FOR...**

*Make a note of four or five people you are specifically praying for. It may be helpful to list their names in your planner so that you remember to pray for them throughout the week.*

○ _____

○ _____

○ _____

○ _____

○ _____

## SCRIPTURE MEDITATION

*The name of the Lord is a strong tower;
the righteous run to it and are protected.*

**PROVERBS 18:10**

▶ *Reflect on what this verse tells you about who God is.*

▶ *Think about what this verse tells you about who you are.*

▶ *Write this verse in your planner, or put it in a place
where you will see it frequently. Throughout the week,
consider how it should affect the way you live.*

## GRATITUDE

*Reflect on the ways God has shown His faithfulness to you
over the last week. List five things you are thankful for.*

1. _____

2. _____

3. _____

4. _____

5. _____

## SPIRITUAL GROWTH | FAST

*Consider fasting from something this week in order to focus on your need for God. What could you fast from? What would be the duration and frequency of your fast? Make a plan for how you will replace your fasted item with the pursuit of God and His Word.*

## WEEK-AT-A-GLANCE CHECKLIST

*Whatever you do, do it from the heart, as something done for the Lord and not for people, knowing that you will receive the reward of an inheritance from the Lord. You serve the Lord Christ.*
*—Colossians 3:23-24*

- ○ **MAKE A PLAN FOR WHEN YOU WILL PRAY AND READ YOUR BIBLE THIS WEEK.**

- ○ **ADD ANY UPCOMING EVENTS TO YOUR CALENDAR.**

- ○ **JOT DOWN A TO-DO LIST OF TASKS THAT MUST BE COMPLETED THIS WEEK.**

- ○ **MAKE A NOTE OF YOUR TOP THREE PRIORITIES THIS WEEK TO STAY ON TRACK.**

## GOSPEL-CENTERED AFFIRMATION

*In the mighty name of the Lord, I find safety.*

WEEK 52

## JOURNAL

*When planning a week, it is common to think of our to-do lists, but do we also consider the state of our souls? Take a moment to journal about your fears, joys, worries, desires, and stressors.*

## PRAYER

*Use the following prayer prompts to have a conversation with God about the week ahead.*

▶ **LORD, YOU ARE...**

▶ **LORD, I FEEL...**

▶ **LORD, HELP ME WITH...**

▶ **LORD, FORGIVE ME FOR...**

*Make a note of four or five people you are specifically praying for. It may be helpful to list their names in your planner so that you remember to pray for them throughout the week.*

○ _____

○ _____

○ _____

○ _____

○ _____

## SCRIPTURE MEDITATION

*Therefore, let us approach the throne of grace
with boldness, so that we may receive mercy
and find grace to help us in time of need.*
**HEBREWS 4:16**

▶ *Reflect on what this verse tells you about who God is.*

▶ *Think about what this verse tells you about who you are.*

▶ *Write this verse in your planner, or put it in a place
where you will see it frequently. Throughout the week,
consider how it should affect the way you live.*

## GRATITUDE

*Reflect on the ways God has shown His faithfulness to you
over the last week. List five things you are thankful for.*

1. _____

2. _____

3. _____

4. _____

5. _____

## SPIRITUAL GROWTH | FELLOWSHIP

*Plan a time to fellowship with friends this week. Go ahead and reach out to them now to get it on the calendar!*

## WEEK-AT-A-GLANCE CHECKLIST

*Whatever you do, do it from the heart, as something done for the Lord and not for people, knowing that you will receive the reward of an inheritance from the Lord. You serve the Lord Christ.*
*— Colossians 3:23-24*

○ MAKE A PLAN FOR WHEN YOU WILL PRAY
  AND READ YOUR BIBLE THIS WEEK.

○ ADD ANY UPCOMING EVENTS TO
  YOUR CALENDAR.

○ JOT DOWN A TO-DO LIST OF TASKS THAT
  MUST BE COMPLETED THIS WEEK.

○ MAKE A NOTE OF YOUR TOP THREE
  PRIORITIES THIS WEEK TO STAY ON TRACK.

## GOSPEL-CENTERED AFFIRMATION

*In Jesus, I will find gracious
help at the throne of God.*